1 MONTH OF FREE READING

at

www.ForgottenBooks.com

By purchasing this book you are eligible for one month membership to ForgottenBooks.com, giving you unlimited access to our entire collection of over 1,000,000 titles via our web site and mobile apps.

To claim your free month visit:

www.forgottenbooks.com/free956957

* Offer is valid for 45 days from date of purchase. Terms and conditions apply.

ISBN 978-0-260-57211-0
PIBN 10956957

This book is a reproduction of an important historical work. Forgotten Books uses state-of-the-art technology to digitally reconstruct the work, preserving the original format whilst repairing imperfections present in the aged copy. In rare cases, an imperfection in the original, such as a blemish or missing page, may be replicated in our edition. We do, however, repair the vast majority of imperfections successfully; any imperfections that remain are intentionally left to preserve the state of such historical works.

Forgotten Books is a registered trademark of FB &c Ltd.
Copyright © 2018 FB &c Ltd.
FB &c Ltd, Dalton House, 60 Windsor Avenue, London, SW19 2RR.
Company number 08720141. Registered in England and Wales.

For support please visit www.forgottenbooks.com

NISTIR 7255

Data and Informatics Needs in Biomaterials

Charles P. Sturrock

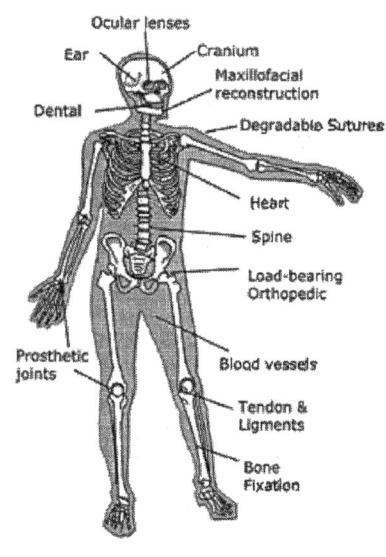

Data and Informatics Needs in Biomaterials

Charles P. Sturrock
Ceramics Division
Materials Science and Engineering Laboratory

September 2005

U.S. DEPARTMENT OF COMMERCE
Carlos M. Gutierrez, Secretary
TECHNOLOGY ADMINISTRATION
Michelle O'Neill, Acting Under Secretary of Commerce for Technology
NATIONAL INSTITUTE OF STANDARDS AND TECHNOLOGY
William Jeffrey, Director

Certain commercial equipment, instruments, or materials are identified in this document to specify adequately experimental procedures and conditions. Such identification does not imply recommendation or endorsement by the National Institute of Standards and Technology, nor does it imply that the materials, software, or equipment identified are necessarily the best available for the purpose.

Data and Informatics Needs in Biomaterials

Objective

The principal objective of this study was, as its name implies, to identify data and informatics needs in biomaterials. What are "biomaterials"? A commonly accepted definition of this term is:

"A biomaterial is a nonviable material used in a medical device, intended to interact with biological systems." (Williams, 1987)

So biomaterials are natural or artificial materials that are used to replace, or augment the function of, living tissue. If the word "nonviable" is removed, the definition is broadened and can address tissue engineering and hybrid artificial organ applications where living cells are used.

Why study biomaterials? Because biomedical devices and the materials from which they are made represent one of the fastest-growing segments of both the biotechnology and materials industries. A 1989 report (Anon., 1989) estimated annual U.S. biomaterials industry sales of over $50 billion and an annual growth rate of 13%. By 2002 the total U.S. medical device market stood at $77 billion, with global sales estimated at 2 to 3 times this figure (Ratner, 2004b). To date the consumers of biomaterials are disproportionately older people, as the majority of intraocular lenses, heart valves, pacemakers, coronary/vascular stents, and joint prostheses (primarily hip and knee) have been implanted in people over 60 years of age. The large numbers of Americans born in the two decades following World War II will turn 60 over the next twenty years. Similar demographics apply in other industrialized countries. Furthermore, the use of biomaterials in younger people is increasing, along with the increase in the useful life of biomedical devices: for example, hip and knee joint prostheses used to be considered successful if they lasted 10 years; now 15 years or even 20 years is not uncommon. Both basic demographics and advances in the useful life of biomedical implants indicate a robust growth in the biomaterials industry for the foreseeable future.

What distinguishes biomaterials from other materials applications? The last phrase of the above definition of biomaterials, i.e., "... intended to interact with biological systems.", identifies the distinguishing feature of biomaterials, and introduces the critical role of the *biocompatibility* of biomaterials, which has been defined:

"Biocompatibility is the ability of a material to perform with an appropriate host response in a specific application." (Williams, 1987)

Examples of "appropriate host responses" include the formation of a natural layer of cells encapsulating bioinert materials such as aluminum oxide, the osseointegration of bioactive materials such as hydroxyapatite or Bioglass, or the complete resorption of biodegradable materials such as calcium phosphate and lactic- and glycolic acid copolymers. The critical issue of biocompatibility is what sets biomaterials apart from much of materials science and engineering: any prospective new biomaterial must be proven to be biocompatible before consideration for use.

Turning to the issue of biomaterials data and informatics, there are four main requirements which must be fulfilled by biomaterials: corrosion resistance, biocompatibility, bioadhesion, and biofunctionality (Black, 1998). Considering the test methods used to determine these requirements, only the measurement of mechanical properties, including fatigue (i.e., biofunctionality) supplies objectively comparable results because the relevant test methods have been standardized. In the investigation of corrosion resistance, biocompatibility, and bioadhesion, the absence or decline of standardization has led to idiosyncratic or divergent test methods; hence the results of such tests are not comparable. The net conclusion is that a standardization effort is required before undertaking all but very narrow informatics efforts in the areas of corrosion resistance, biocompatibility, and bioadhesion. Only biofunctionality research conducted according to established standards has yielded objectively comparable data that lend themselves to informatics drawn from multiple sources.

With these definitions and basic principles established, the objective of this effort was refined to examine the current state of biomaterials property data and informatics and identify needs for future related work.

Scope

In this study we included all biomaterials, whether from natural sources, such as cellulose, catgut or silk, or engineered materials, including: ceramics, metals, polymers, and composites. We did not include bioengineered devices that are simply in contact with the skin, such as hearing aids and wearable artificial limbs.

Because of the paucity of standards in the areas of corrosion resistance, biocompatibility, and bioadhesion, primarily biofunctionality data, quantifying mechanical properties of biomaterials, were examined. The properties included strengths and moduli derived from forces applied in: tension, compression, bending, and torsion. Hardness, fatigue, fracture toughness, and wear data were also examined.

In addition to the literature on the mechanical properties of biomaterials, general biomaterials review articles were also surveyed, along with articles on subjects related to biomaterials, such as: needs of the industry, availability, biocompatibility, education, nanotechnology, standardization, surface science, and tissue engineering.

Electronic sources consulted included the Internet, including several online journals, the Web of Science bibliographic database, and several online structure and property databases. Hard-copy sources included books, and scientific, engineering and trade journals.

Approach

We began by conducting library searches for items under the subject headings "biomaterials" and "data". We quickly found (Black, 1998), and (Ratner, 1996) [which was succeeded by a second edition (Ratner, 2004b)]. The first of these sources is entitled *Handbook of Biomaterials Properties*. This 616-page handbook draws together much of the accepted data and information on the materials aspect of both implantable materials and natural tissues and fluids, broadly distributed in various publications, with varying degrees of accuracy and precision. The book addresses the intrinsic and interactive properties of biomaterials, as well as their applications and historical context.

The second of these sources is the principal textbook in the field, and in the second edition comprises 851 very dense pages of up-to-date comprehensive reviews of all aspects of biomaterials. An historical perspective of materials engineering principles is integrated with the biological interactions of biomaterials, regulatory and ethical issues and future directions of the field, and a state-of-the-art update of medical and biotechnological applications. Contributions detailing the principles of cell biology, immunology, and pathology have been integrated into this edition. The chapters focus on the clinical uses of biomaterials as components in implants, devices, and artificial organs and their uses in biotechnology as well as the characterization of the physical, chemical, biochemical and surface properties of these materials.

Both of these books contain extensive bibliographies, which identify other relevant books, journal articles, web sites, and standards. A total of 21 other books were identified as having information relevant to this study. The cited articles spanned dozens of journals, including those of general science, materials science and engineering, biomedical sciences, and the clinical professions. The cited standards were all developed by Committee F04 on Medical and Surgical Materials and Devices of the American Society for Testing and Materials (ASTM).

Several months were spent visiting online sources of relevant information. Commercial search engines and the Web of Science were used, respectively, to find web sites and journal articles that addressed "biomaterials properties (or data)" or "biomedical materials properties (or data)". Several hundred web sites were visited, and about 40 were identified as having useful information for the purposes of this study.

The journal articles found in this manner were downloaded when available in full online; in cases where only an abstract was available online, a copy of the entire article was obtained from the print edition of the relevant journal. Of the resources examined, not surprisingly the web sites had the greatest variability in quality of the information presented, no doubt a consequence of the absence of peer review for most of that information.

After the journal articles, web content, and biomaterials standards were compiled, the following organization scheme emerged (number of articles + web sites + standards in parentheses):
- Biomaterials: Data and Other Needs (19)
- Biomaterials: General (60)
- Biomaterials: Other (e.g., Availability, Biocompatibility, Education, Nanotechnology, Standardization, Surface Science, Tissue Engineering) (36)
- Ceramics (31)
- Metals (31)
- Polymers (36)
- Composites (30)
- ASTM Biomaterials Standards (33)

Given that the literature survey began with the only handbook and the definitive textbook on the subject of biomaterials, and also included exhaustive Internet and literature searches of relevant subject matter, we assert that a comprehensive survey of existing biomaterials data and informatics has been achieved, and the accumulated references comprise a representative sampling of available knowledge of the field.

Assessment – Broad Picture

The key players in biomaterials are academic researchers. Also important are medical practitioners from many specialties, including: orthopedics, ophthalmology, cardiology, dentistry, dermatology, surgery, and many others. These individuals are perhaps most easily reached through their respective professional societies: in the former case, research societies such as the Society for Biomaterials, Orthopedic Research Society, Society for Vascular Surgery, etc.; in the latter case, medical societies such as the American Medical Association, the American Dental Association, the American Academy of Orthopaedic Surgeons, the American College of Cardiology, etc. In addition to these U.S.-based societies, corresponding societies exist throughout Europe and Japan.

There are two government agencies in the U.S. of importance regarding biomaterials. The Food and Drug Administration (FDA) must approve any biomedical device used in the United States. The National Institutes of Health (NIH), primarily through its National Institute of Biomedical Imaging and Bioengineering, funds much of the academic biomedical materials research. The NIH is also responsible for guidelines for the proper care and use of laboratory animals and for oversight of that care. Institutions found to be noncompliant with the *Guide for the Care and Use of Laboratory Animals* (NRC, 1996), which is funded by the NIH, can be penalized by having funding support withdrawn.

The principal industrial players in biomaterials are the biomedical device manufacturers. In 2002, there were more than 1800 types of products marketed as medical devices with 60 000 to 80 000 brands and models (Anon, 2002). In 2003, there were 13 000 registered U.S. medical device manufacturers employing 300 000 individuals (Ratner, 2004b).

Finally, certainly the largest stakeholder group, and perhaps the most interested, consists of the consumers of biomaterials. In 2000, it was estimated that 8% to 10% of Americans had a permanent medical implant (Anon, 2002). Based on the 2000 U.S. Census, this estimate yields a range of 22.5 million to 28.1 million Americans with a medical implant. These figures do not include the number of Americans who wear contact lenses, which is unknown but can be estimated at 15 million from the 30 million contact lenses sold in the U.S. in 2000 (Ratner, 2004b). So somewhere around 40 million Americans are biomaterials consumers. If in addition to this group we include individuals who have had cavities filled with dental amalgams or other biocompatible materials, along with those who have had accidental or surgical wounds closed with sutures, plus persons who swallow tablets or capsules with polymeric coatings, then virtually every American is a consumer of biomaterials at some point in his or her life. For other industrialized countries in which there is good access to healthcare, including modern ophthalmology and dentistry, a similar overwhelming majority of the population consumes biomaterials. In developing countries, the percentages of biomaterials consumers are smaller, but this is largely due to poorer standards of living and the corresponding lack of access to modern medicine.

The Internet is a useful indicator of the number of organizations involved with biomaterials. The web site www.biomat.net lists over 100 organizations with web sites that are "biomaterials-oriented". The organizations include biomaterials professional societies, industrial associations and consortia, and research institutes and foundations. The same web site also separately includes a page devoted to biomaterials research organizations, with over 200 listed for the U.S. alone, primarily university departments. The U.S. entries account for about one-third of the total shown on this list.

The facilities devoted to the research of the mechanical properties of biomaterials are little different from those found in materials science and engineering laboratories, and usually include mechanical test equipment, light and electron microscopes. Universal testing machines that can be configured for tensile, flexural, compression, torsion, or fatigue tests are ubiquitous, and require an investment of approximately $20,000 to $50,000, fully equipped. Microscopy instrumentation varies greatly in methodology, power and price. For example, the range of magnification available in light microscopy is from about 5x to about 1000x. Because of the much smaller wavelength of electrons, as compared to visible light, the maximum magnification for electron microscopy is considerably higher: scanning electron microscopes can magnify objects up to 300,000 times, and transmission electron microscopes can magnify objects up to 1,000,000 times. The corresponding microscope prices also vary considerably: about $100 to $2,000 for an optical microscope, while electron microscopes sell for about $50,000 to $250,000.

Much of biomaterials research involves the methods of surface science (Castner, 2002). The common methods used to characterize biomaterials surfaces include: electron spectroscopy for chemical analysis (ESCA), in which X-rays are used to induce the emission of electrons of characteristic energy; Auger electron spectroscopy (AES), in which a focused electron beam stimulates the emission of Auger electrons; secondary ion mass spectrometry (SIMS), in which ion bombardment sputters secondary ions from the surface; Fourier transform infrared (FTIR) spectrometry, attenuated total reflectance (ATR) mode, in which infrared radiation is adsorbed and excites molecular vibrations; scanning tunneling microscopy (STM), which involves measurement of the quantum tunneling current between a metal tip and a conductive surface; atomic force microscopy (AFM), which involves measurement of the deflection of a tip mounted on a flexible cantilever arm; and scanning electron microscopy (SEM), which involves the imaging of secondary electron emission induced by a focused electron beam. The cost of the associated equipment varies greatly: for FTIR-ATR, STM, AFM and SEM, prices range from $5,000 to $100,000, whereas ESCA, AES, and SIMS require an investment in excess of $100,000.

Finally, as a consequence of the unique biocompatibility requirements of biomaterials, facilities are needed for the care and housing of laboratory animals used as subjects for *in vivo* studies. Requirements of these facilities are spelled out in the aforementioned *Guide for the Care and Use of Laboratory Animals* (NRC, 1996), which includes provisions for housing, handling, veterinary care, and euthanasia.

As stated above, the general topics of biomaterials research are: corrosion resistance, biocompatibility, bioadhesion, and biofunctionality. The subject of biomaterials mechanical properties is included under biofunctionality studies, as elucidation of these properties provides insights on how biomaterials will function in a biological environment. Corrosion resistance is considered broadly, and includes not only the dissolution of pure metals and alloys used in biomedical applications, but also the degradation of the properties of ceramic and polymer biomaterials exposed *in vitro* or *in vivo*. Biocompatibility studies examine the biological response to the presence of biomaterials, and bioadhesion research focuses on the challenging problem of binding biomaterials to natural tissues.

There is relatively little coordination of biomaterials research. The only biomaterials standards currently maintained are for the compositional specification of certain well-established biomaterials, and for the measurement of some mechanical properties. The biomaterials-related professional societies publish journals for documenting research results and organize conferences and symposia for presentation of these results, but there does not seem to be any kind of effort originating within these societies at coordinating the research, either inter- or intra-society. The impetus for the modest efforts at coordination of biomaterials research that have been made thus far seems to have come from FDA, NIH and NIST. NIH has sponsored workshops on biomaterials research needs and opportunities (Eisenberger, 1996), (Barenberg, 1991), and with FDA on medical implant information, performance, and policies (Anon, 2002). NIST has sponsored workshops addressing reference biomaterials needs (Tesk, 2000), reference data needs (Tesk, 2001), and standards for biomedical materials and devices (Anon, 2001). The workshop reports summarize the status of the fields and provide recommendations for the biomaterials community. These recommendations will be addressed further in a subsequent section.

Assessment – Issues and Needs

The broad categories of biomaterials research are: corrosion resistance, biocompatibility, bioadhesion, and biofunctionality. Different issues arise according to the category, and to the class of biomaterial: whether metal, ceramic, polymer, carbon and composite, or biologically-derived. Each class of biomaterial is addressed in turn, with example applications provided along with relevant issues.

Metals are widely used as load-bearing implants due to their strength and toughness. Implant metals include: type 316L stainless steel, cobalt-chromium-molybdenum alloys, titanium and its alloys, tantalum, nickel-titanium alloy, and precious metals gold, silver, and platinum. Metals are susceptible to degradation by corrosion, a process that not only diminishes their mechanical properties, but can also release by-products (such as ions, chemical compounds, and particulate debris) that may cause adverse biological responses. Metals depend on a stable passivation layer (~10 nm) of oxide to provide corrosion resistance. Biomedical applications of metals include hip and knee prostheses, fracture fixation wires, pins, screws, and plates, dental prostheses, coronary stents, pacemaker leads and even sutures.

The primary biomaterials research issues surrounding metals include:
- Electrochemical corrosion and durability of the passive layer
- Nonelectrochemical degradative mechanisms including protein/metal interactions
- Hypersensitivity and immune reactions
- Interaction with biological pathways
- "Stress-shielding" – bone loss due to preferential loading through metallic prostheses

Ceramics are inorganic materials that are stiff, hard, and chemically stable. They are often used in circumstances where wear resistance is vital. The main problem with ceramic components is that they are relatively brittle and difficult to process. Of the large number of ceramics known only a few are suitably biocompatible. These "bioceramics" can be grouped according to their relative reactivity in physiological environments: bioinert, bioactive, and bioresorbable.

Bioinert ceramics elicit minimal response from host tissue, which generally treats such ceramics as a foreign body by encapsulation within a layer of cells. As the name implies, bioinert ceramics undergo little physical/chemical alteration *in vivo*, in other words, they are extremely stable. They have high compressive strength and excellent wear resistance. However, they can be brittle and subject to fracture from tensile, shear, or torsional forces. Examples of bioinert ceramics include alumina (Al_2O_3), partially stabilized zirconia (ZrO_2), and silicon nitride (Si_3N_4). Example applications include the femoral head of total hip replacements, and single crystal (sapphire) dental implants.

The primary research issues are:
- Degradation mechanisms, e.g., crack propagation due to preferential dissolution of impurities
  Durability

- Fracture toughness
- Surface activity

Bioactive ceramics are designed to induce a specific biological activity; in most cases one that will give a strong bonding to bone. The interface between a bioactive ceramic and bone is often so strong that removal of an implant necessitates breaking the surrounding bone or, in some cases, the implant (Rawlings, 1993). Examples of bioactive ceramics include Bioglass ($Na_2OCaOP_2O_3$-SiO), and hydroxyapatite ($Ca_{10}(PO_4)_6(OH)_2$) sintered at high temperature. Applications include bone cement for dental and maxillofacial reconstruction, and bioactive coatings on metallic implants for tissue ingrowth.

The primary research issues are:
- Mechanisms responsible for bioactivity
- Compositional dependence of bioactivity bonding to bone and soft tissue
- Effect of elastic modulus mismatch on stress transfer
- Effect of bioelectric potentials on interfacial bonding
- Long-term stability of bioactive interfacial bonding
- Long-term fatigue resistance of bioactive coatings and composites

Bioresorbable (sometimes called biodegradable) ceramics are materials that degrade by hydrolytic breakdown in the body while they are being replaced by regenerating natural tissue; the chemical by-products of the degrading materials are absorbed and released via metabolic processes of the body. The dissolution rate is controlled by composition and surface area (density). Examples of bioresorbable ceramics include calcium sulfate (Plaster of Paris – $CaSO_4 \cdot \frac{1}{2}H_2O$), tricalcium phosphate ($Ca_3(PO_4)_2$), hydroxyapatite ($Ca_{10}(PO_4)_6(OH)_2$) sintered at low temperature, and other calcium phosphate salts. Applications include temporary bone space fillers for orthopedic, dental, and maxillofacial prostheses, and temporary scaffolds for tissue engineering.

The relevant issues are:
- How to measure bioabsorption and effect of tissue site
- Calcification enhancement
- Biologic effects of degradation products
- Biologic pathways that interact with degradation products and effect on these pathways
- How to assess effects of enzymes on degradability
- Effects of processing and sterilization with labile release agents incorporated into the ceramic
- Effects/control on wound healing and bone formation
- When is a material a device and when is it a drug
- Reluctance of industry to sponsor new biodegradables for controlled release because of regulatory cost

Polymers are organic materials consisting of large macromolecules composed of many repeating units. They represent the largest class of biomaterials (Cooper, 2004), and are the materials of choice for most cardiovascular devices as well as for replacement and augmentation of various soft tissues. Polymers are also used in drug delivery systems, in diagnostic aids, and as a scaffolding material for tissue engineering applications. Example applications include vascular grafts, heart valves, artificial hearts, breast implants, contact and intraocular lenses, dialyzers and plasmapheresis units, coatings for pharmaceuticals, sutures, adhesives, and blood substitutes. A few examples of polymers and their uses are given in Table 1.

Applications	Polymer(s)
Cardiovascular implants	Polyethylene; poly(vinyl chloride); polyester; silicone rubber; poly(ethylene terephthalate); polytetrafluoroethylene
Orthopedic implants	Ultra-high-molecular-weight polyethylene; poly(methyl methacrylate)
Contact and intraocular lenses	Hydrogels; poly(methyl methacrylate); poly(2-hydroxyethyl methacrylate); poly(ethylene glycol dimethacrylate)
Drug release	Poly(lactide-*co*-glycolide); poly(anhydride)
Tissue engineering	Poly(lactic acid); poly(glycolic acid); poly(lactide-*co*-glycolide)
Absorbable sutures	Poly(glycolide); 10/90 poly(L-lactide-*co*-glycolide); poly(p-dioxanone); poly(alkylene oxalate)
Tissue adhesives	Cyanoacrylates; gelatin/resorcinol; fibrin glue and subclass of hemostatic agents which include collagen, gelatin foam, succinylated amylase, and oxidized regenerated cellulose

Table 1 – Biomedical applications of polymers

The mechanical and thermal behavior of polymers is influenced by several factors, including the composition of the polymer backbone and side groups, the structure of the chains, and the molecular weight of the molecules. Plastic deformation occurs when the applied mechanical forces cause the macromolecular chains to slide past one another. Changes in polymer composition or structure that increase resistance to relative movement of the chains increase the strength and decrease the plasticity of the material. Substitutions into the backbone that increase its rigidity hinder movement of the chains. Increasing macromolecule length (molecular weight) also makes the chains less mobile and hinders their relative movement. Polymers may also degrade in physiological environments, a process which is exploited in many biomedical applications, including drug delivery, tissue engineering, absorbable sutures, and tissue adhesives.

Synthetic polymers may contain various (often unspecified) additives, traces of catalysts, inhibitors, and other chemical compounds needed for their synthesis. Over time in the physiological environment, these compounds can leach from the polymer surface. As with the by-products released from the corrosion of metallic implants, the chemicals released from polymers may induce adverse local and systemic host reactions that cause clinical complications. This release is a concern for materials, such as bone cement, that are polymerized in the body and for flexible polymers, such as poly(vinyl chloride), that contain low-molecular-weight species (plasticizers) to make them pliable.

With respect to mechanical properties, compared with metals and ceramics, polymers have much lower strengths and moduli but they can be deformed to a greater extent before failure. Consequently, with the exception of ultra-high-molecular-weight polyethylene, polymers are generally not used in biomedical applications that bear loads.

The primary issues for nondegradable polymers are:
- Instability to gamma radiation
- Reactivity with certain classes of drugs
- Lack of pharmaceutical grade
- Lot-to-lot variability
- Tissue compatibility
- Hydrolytic stability
- Calcification
- Risk assessment of additives, low molecular weight components, *in vivo* degradation products, sterilization
- Long-term performance/functionality
- Lack of database to assess bulk and surface properties, additives, soft tissue reactivity, blood interaction, mutagenicity/carcinogenicity/tumorigenesis and sterilizability
- Improved understanding of *in vivo* interactions, role of material surface chemistry and morphological properties in thrombus formation, protein and cell consumption, and embolus formation
- Lack of standards

The primary issues for bioresorbable and soluble polymers are:
- How to measure bioabsorbability and effect of tissue site
- Biological effects of degradation products
- Biologic pathways that interact with degradation products and effect on these pathways
- How to assess effects of enzymes on degradability
- Surface vs. bulk erosion
- Effect of processing and sterilization on biodegradation/bioabsorption
- Processing and sterilization with labile release agents incorporated into the polymer
- Effects/control of wound healing
- When is a material a device and when is it a drug
- Reluctance of industry to sponsor new biodegradables for controlled release because of regulatory cost

The primary issues for polymeric tissue adhesives are:
- Chemical and mechanical biocompatibility
- Strength and durability of adhered surfaces
- Tissue adhesions
- Biologic effects of degradation products
- Biologic pathways that interact with degradation products and effect on these pathways
- Effects of processing and sterilization on biodegradation
- Effects/control of wound healing

Carbons and composite materials are grouped together herein because as a biomaterial, elemental carbon is most often used in composite applications, such as a coating on heart valve components, or as a fiber in carbon fiber-reinforced ultra-high molecular weight polyethylene for orthopedic applications. Composites are materials consisting of two or more chemically distinct constituents, on a macroscale, having a distinct interface separating them (Migliaresi, 2004). Hence composites consist of one or more discontinuous phases embedded within a continuous phase. Most composite materials are fabricated to provide desired mechanical properties such as strength, stiffness, toughness, and fatigue resistance. Biomaterial composite applications include arterial prostheses, intervertebral disks duplicating the natural structure, bone fixation plates and nails with controlled stiffness, biodegradable scaffolds for bone regeneration, prosthetic hip stems, artificial tooth roots, bone cements, acetabular cups, artificial tendons and ligaments, and bone filling/regeneration applications.

The research issues of importance to carbons and composite biomaterials are:
- Characterization
- Strength
- Fracture toughness
- Measurement of bioactivity *in vitro* and *in vivo*
- Effects of sterilization

Biologically-derived biomaterials originate from natural sources, including human, animal, and plant tissues. Examples of natural polymers include: proteins such as silk, keratin, collagen, gelatin, fibrinogen, elastin, actin, and myosin; polysaccharides such as cellulose, amylase, dextran, chitin, and glycosaminoglycans; and polynucleotides such as deoxy- and ribonucleic acids. Collagen is perhaps the most frequently used biologically-derived biomaterial, with applications such as sutures, blood vessels (bovine carotid artery, human umbilical vein), heart valves (processed porcine heart valve), tendons, ligaments, dermal regeneration, and drug-delivery systems.

The issues surrounding biologically-derived biomaterials include:
- Ethics
- Chronic, low-level antigenic responses
- Purity
- Long-term durability
- Calcification

To summarize this brief overview, a schematic of the human body and examples of biomaterials applications is found in Figure 1.

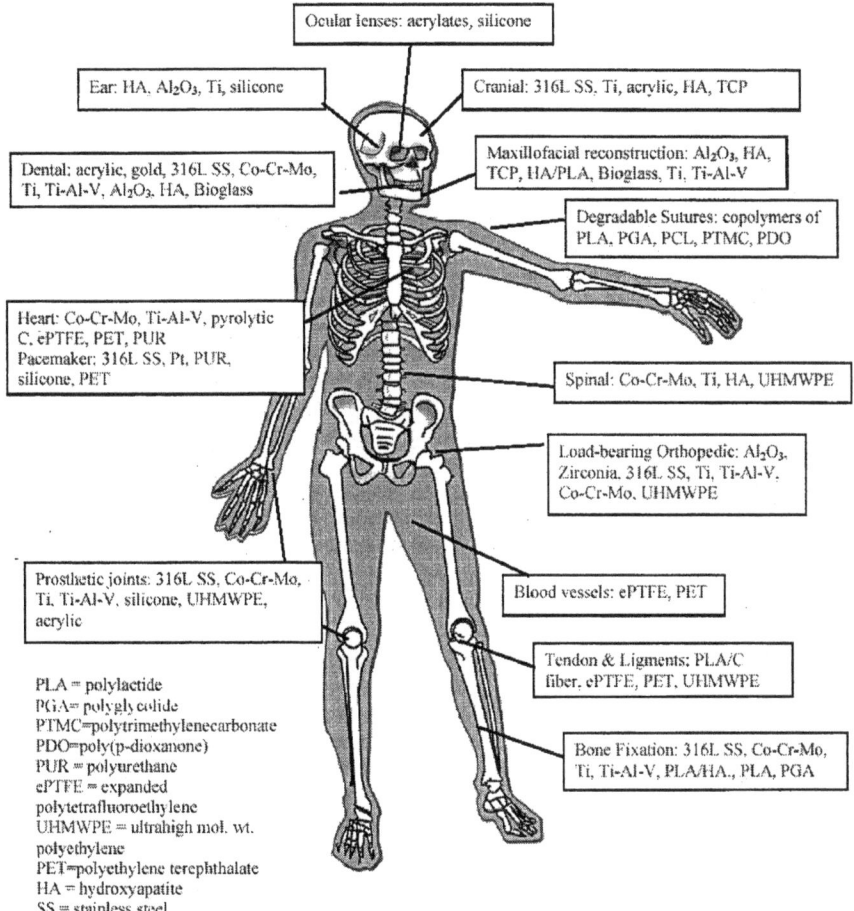

Figure 1 – Biomaterials applications. Figure provided courtesy of MIT Open Course Ware.

Existing data and informatics

Existing biomaterials data are widely scattered across the relevant literature and the Internet; a smaller portion of proprietary data is maintained by medical device manufacturers. The *Handbook of Biomaterial Properties* (Black, 1998), at 616 pages, is the primary printed reference. Other handbook data can be found in: (Engelberg, 1991 (polymer data only)), (Park, 1992), (Park, 1995), (Donachie, 1998), and (Ratner, 2004b).

Regarding biomaterials informatics, there is one known online collection of biomaterials property data. By contrast, there are several online collections of biomolecular structural data. The former and three examples of the latter are described.

Sponsored and hosted by the University of Michigan School of Dentistry, the *Biomaterials Properties Database* (O'Brien, 1997b) is a collection of property data drawn from 244 printed references. The data are updated periodically from a printed handbook of dental materials properties (O'Brien, 1997a). Interestingly, although the web site includes a request for additional data submissions, the latest revision is dated April 1997.

The data are organized by material property into 45 tables (Table 2):

1. Bond Strength Between Restorative Materials and Tooth Structures	
2. Brinell Hardness Number	24. Poisson's Ratio
3. Coefficient of Friction	25. Proportional Limit
4. Coefficient of Thermal Expansion (Linear)	26. Shear Strength
5. Color Range of Natural Teeth	27. Shore A Hardness
6. Colors of Dental Shade Guides	28. Solubility and Disintegration in Water
7. Contact Angle	29. Specific Heat
8. Creep of Amalgam	30. Strain in Compression
9. Critical Surface Tension	31. Surface Free Energy
10. Density	32. Surface Tension
11. Dynamic Modulus	33. Tear Energy
12. Elastic Modulus	34. Tear Strength
13. Flow	35. Thermal Conductivity
14. Heat of Fusion	36. Thermal Diffusivity
15. Heat of Reaction	37. Transverse Strength
16. Impact Strength, IZOD	38. Ultimate Compressive Strength
17. Index of Refraction	39. Ultimate Tensile Strength
18. Knoop Hardness Number	40. Vapor Pressure
19. Melting Temperatures and Ranges	41. Vickers Hardness
20. Mohs' Hardness	42. Viscosity
21. Penetration Coefficient	43. Water Sorption
22. Percent Elongation	44. Yield Strength
23. Permanent Deformation	45. Zeta Potential

Table 2 – Data tables in the *Biomaterial Properties Database*

After one of these properties has been selected, the next screen displays the relevant table containing all available data sorted by material for the property chosen. Despite its inclusive name, the *Biomaterials Properties Database* emphasizes dental materials, as revealed by some of the names of the data tables (e.g., "Color Range of Natural Teeth", "Colors of Dental Shade Guides", "Creep of Amalgam", etc.) and by the reference list, which is dominated by citations from the dental materials literature.

Turning to biomolecular structural data, there are several relevant online databases. Three examples are discussed briefly herein. The first of these is the *Nucleic Acid Database* (NDB – Berman, 2002). As its name suggests, the NDB is a repository of three-dimensional structural information about nucleic acids, including deoxyribonucleic acid (DNA) and ribonucleic acid (RNA), the basic hereditary material in all cells that contain all the information necessary to make proteins. The NDB is supported by funds from the National Science Foundation and the Department of Energy, and is operated by Rutgers, The State University of New Jersey. Begun in 1992, the NDB presently contains 2655 available structures.

A second source of biomolecular structural data is the *Biological Macromolecule Crystallization Database* (BMCD – Gilliland, 1994). Sponsored by the National Aeronautics and Space Administration (NASA) and

NIST, and hosted by NIST, the BMCD contains crystal data and the relevant crystallization conditions. Begun in the 1980s, the current version of the BMCD contains 3547 crystal entries from 2526 biological macromolecules for which diffraction quality crystals have been obtained. These include proteins, protein:protein complexes, nucleic acids, nucleic acid:nucleic acid complexes, protein:nucleic acid complexes, and viruses. In addition to including crystallization data reported in the literature, the BMCD contains the NASA Protein Crystal Growth Archive, which includes the crystallization data generated from studies carried out in a microgravity environment supported by NASA. Data from other crystallization experiments carried out under microgravity sponsored by other international space agencies are also included.

By far the largest structural database on biological molecules is the *Protein Data Bank* (PDB – Berman, 2000). Begun in 1971 with seven original structures at the Brookhaven National Laboratory, the PDB is one of the oldest biological databases of any kind. Presently it is operated by the Research Collaboratory for Structural Bioinformatics, whose members include: Rutgers, The State University of New Jersey; the San Diego Supercomputer Center at the University of California, San Diego; and the Department of Biochemistry at the University of Wisconsin-Madison. The PDB is supported by funds from the National Science Foundation, the National Institute of General Medical Sciences, the Office of Science, Department of Energy, the National Library of Medicine, the National Cancer Institute, the National Center for Research Resources, the National Institute of Biomedical Imaging and Bioengineering, and the National Institute of Neurological Disorders and Stroke. The PDB is the single worldwide repository for the processing and distribution of 3-D structure data of large molecules of proteins and nucleic acids. Structural data are submitted continuously and new releases are issued weekly. As of 13 September 2005 there were 32 598 structures contained in the PDB.

The BMCD, NDB, and PDB are all examples of the burgeoning field of structural bioinformatics, which presently exists at the fringes of traditional biomedical materials research. However, as we shall see below, the presence of nucleic acids, proteins and other biomolecules on biomaterials surfaces greatly influences the biocompatibility of implants, so these data will eventually play a critical and potentially pivotal role in the future of biomaterials science and engineering.

The data from these printed and electronic sources are used to characterize biomaterials, to design biomedical devices, to screen or select materials for biomedical applications, to simulate biomaterial performance, to develop protocols for the synthesis of biological macromolecules, and to substantiate hypotheses and theory.

Desired data and informatics

Over the years there have been several panels established and workshops conducted for the purpose of articulating the needs and opportunities in biomaterials and related subjects. A review of the ensuing publications illustrates the evolution of these needs and opportunities. Table 3 provides a summary.

Year	Panel/Event	Data/informatics needed
1986	Committee on Materials Science and Engineering	Evaluated materials property data for design
1988	Biomaterials Advisory Panel	Database that will address standardized measures of: • Material/blood, material/soft tissue, and material/organ interactions; • Surface characterization; • *In vivo* material stability; • Bioactivity; • Fatigue resistance; • Implant-interface bonding; and • Material reference standards. National center to develop a comprehensive database on the physical, surface,

		and biological properties of biomaterials
1995	NIH Biomaterial and Medical Implant Workshop	Central resource of databases relating to materials and devices to provide uniform information on: material and device performance, patient acceptance, animal test results, modes of failure, and long-term survival information
1998	NIST Reference Biomaterials Workshop	(Reference biomaterials needs only articulated)
2000	NIST Biomaterials Reference Data Workshop	Databases of material properties, biological response, test methods, and clinical performance of biomaterials used in the following applications: • Orthopedic • Cardiovascular • Ophthalmic • Dental • Tissue-engineered
2001	NIST Workshop on Standards for Biomedical Materials and Devices	NIST and AdvaMed conduct workshops in: • New biocompatibility test methods • Accelerated life tests that can predict clinical performance of biomaterials • Methods for characterization of biomaterials and biomolecules • Standardized test methods for evaluation of the biostability of materials • Effects of sterilization on materials Fifteen action plans for data-related measurements and standards, including: • Develop a standard interface to properties of materials databases • Develop standardized identifiers (tags) for measurements • Develop data interchange standards among biomedical instruments and implant devices • Develop round-robin testing protocols for assuring accuracy and precision of measurements • Identify coordination issues between clinical data standardization and materials and devices biomedical data requirements
2002	Biomaterials and Medical Implant Science (BMIS) Coordinating Committee Workshop	Six overall recommendations: • Establish Internet-based medical implant information and data resources • Develop standard definitions and practices for recovering implants, conducting research, evaluating outcomes, and reporting results • Catalyze a scientific team approach to gather and disseminate a comprehensive description of implant performance • Educate key stakeholders about research on retrieved implants • Publish a peer-reviewed law article that clarifies the medical implant property rights of patients, manufacturers, hospitals, insurers, and other interested parties • Create a central source of general information regarding the medical value, safety, lifetime, and adverse events associated with medical implants

Table 3 – Summary of recent efforts in articulating biomaterials data/informatics needs

Each of the panels and workshops cited in Table 3 are now described in greater detail.
In 1986 the National Research Council established the Committee on Materials Science and Engineering (Committee) to "present a unified view of recent progress and new directions in materials science and engineering and to assess future opportunities and needs." (Anon., 1989). Five separate panels were derived from this Committee to address: research opportunities and needs, exploitation of materials science and engineering for the national welfare, international cooperation and competition, research resources, and

education. Each of the panels submitted detailed reports to the Committee, from which were prepared an extensive report of approximately 300 pages (Anon., 1989). Biomaterials are treated as one of eight industries in which materials science and engineering play a critical role. The other industries are: aerospace, automotive, chemical, electronics, energy, metals, and telecommunications. Materials databases were identified as needed by all eight industries. Additional general needs identified for biomaterials were: high strength to weight, corrosion resistance, efficient processing, near-net-shape forming, prediction of service life, and prediction of physical properties. More specific needs included: nonthrombogenic surfaces (surfaces that do not promote the formation of clots), reproducible quality, stability to sterilization, biocompatibility, hydrolytic stability, bioresorbability, and high purity. The report states that ultimately, there will be a need for biomaterials that duplicate the physical and biological properties of all native tissues of the body. Examples are shown in Table 4.

End Use Application	Biomaterial Need
Burn/wound coverings	Grafts for epithelium cell regeneration
	Release of antibacterials
Cardiovascular implants	Thromboresistant surfaces
	Small-diameter (< 4 mm) vascular grafts
Catheters: cardiovascular, urinary	Thromboresistant skin
	Infection-resistant surfaces
	Nondenuding (able to slip over epithelial tissue without adhering and stripping)
Controlled release	Bioadhesives
	Bioerodable polymers
	Protein delivery
Diabetes	Hybrid artificial organs
Extracorporeal blood	Immobilized chemotherapeutic treatment agents and enzymes for chemotherapy and detoxification
Neural repair	Polymers that induce nerve regeneration
Ophthalmologic	Artificial corneas
	Vitreous implants
Soft tissue reconstruction	Resorbable polymers with concurrent release of bioactive agents
Wound closure	Tissue adhesives

Table 4 – Biomaterials Needs

The role of federal laboratories in general, and NIST in particular, is proposed explicitly in the report as follows:

> "The federal laboratories, **especially the National Institute of Standards and Technology** in its new role, could play a valuable role in establishing test procedures, setting standards, **assembling data collections**, and transferring technology to industry." (emphasis added)

Among the report's concluding findings are the need for: evaluated materials property data for design; the critical collaboration among universities, government laboratories, and, most importantly, industries (in which most of the data are first generated); and the development of widely accessible electronic databases in convenient format.

In 1988 a biomaterials advisory panel was chartered by the National Academy of Sciences and the National Academy of Engineering to address needs and opportunities in materials science and engineering as perceived by the biomaterials industry (Mueller, 1991)(Barenberg, 1991)(Barenberg, 1988). The panel examined the short-term, intermediate, and long-term needs of the industry and how external factors such as regulations, lack of standards, and international competition influenced the industry. The biomaterials industry is comprised of organizations that design, fabricate, and/or manufacture materials that are used in the health and life sciences fields. The end use applications are medical and dental devices, prostheses, personal care/hygiene, diagnostics, drug delivery, and biotechnology systems.

The industry can be segmented as follows:
- Artificial organs – pancreas, kidney (extracorporeal membrane oxygenator);
- Biosensors – *in vivo/in vitro* blood chemistries;
- Biotechnology – process/purification membranes, enzyme or cellular immobilization substrates, cell culture systems (hollow fibers, microencapsulation), fermentation polymers (e.g., poly β-hydroxybutyrate);
- Cardiovascular – vascular grafts, heart valves, artificial hearts;
- Commodity/disposables – catheters (angioplasty), syringes, gowns/gloves;
- Drug delivery/hybrid artificial organs – *in vivo* controlled/sustained release (ocular, uterus), transdermal release, insulin pumps, artificial pancreas, extracorporeal therapy, synthetic oxygen carriers;
- Maxillofacial, dental, ear, nose & throat, cranial – artificial teeth, soft tissue, mandibular augmentation, ossicular replacement and reconstruction, intracochlear and extracochlear prostheses for the profoundly deaf;
- Ophthalmology – contact lenses, intraocular lenses, artificial corneas/intraocular implants, vitreous implants, bioadhesives;
- Orthopedics – artificial joints (hip, knee); artificial bone (ceramic, Bioglass, hydroxyapatite), fixation plates/screws, fixation cements (polymethyl methacrylate), spinal fusion, tendon prostheses, artificial ligaments);
- Packaging – personal care (sanitary napkins, tampons, condoms), diapers, environmentally degradable polymers, parenterals; and
- Wound management – sutures, bioadhesives, dressings, staples, artificial skin, burn dressings.

The biomaterials industry informatics needs were stated quite succinctly in both (Barenberg, 1988) and (Barenberg, 1991) as follows: "The biomedical materials industry needs to develop a database of information that will address standardized measures of:
- Material/blood, material/soft tissue, and material/organ interactions;
- Surface characterization;
- *In vivo* material stability;
- Bioactivity;
- Fatigue resistance;
- Implant-interface bonding; and
- Material reference standards."

Related to this need, under the heading "Resource Needs", we find in (Barenberg, 1991):

> "Particularly needed is a national center to develop a comprehensive database on the physical, surface, and biological properties of materials for use in medicine and biology. A national center would also evaluate and establish standard testing procedures and standard materials for use by the R&D community. It should have an industrial advisory board, as well as an advisory board composed of academic researchers and clinicians. **It should probably be housed either in or under the auspices of NIST** and funded by the FDA and NIH, **as well as by NIST.**" (emphasis added)

On 16-17 October 1995, the National Institutes of Health convened a workshop that brought together over 100 university, industry, and government experts in biomaterials, medical implants, and the clinical sciences (Eisenberger, 1996). The workshop participants were charged with recommending directions that would advance the science of biomaterials and improve the success of medical implants. The workshop attendees were divided into six working groups to focus on the following topic areas: biocompatibility; manufacturing; commercial implant materials; laboratory and clinical evaluations; and device monitoring, retrieval, and databases. Recommendations were integrated from the findings of the six working groups, and can be divided into two categories: (1) scientific priorities leading to full understanding and creation of successful implants, and (2) an implementation strategy to help realize the future potential of the research advances in the field of biomaterials and medical implants.

Recommended scientific priorities included the design and development of biologically based materials, establishment of an enriched scientific basis for determining the performance and quality of implants, and improvements in advanced processing and manufacturing techniques. Articulated needs included the design and development of materials and devices endowed with biological structure and function, new materials that integrate better understanding of the tissue-device interface, and "smart" and self-monitoring materials for cell-based and gene-based therapies. To optimize costs and patient benefit, more efficient methods are needed to assess human acceptance of biomaterials and medical implants, as are more predictive, less-costly *in vivo* and *in vitro* models. Developing these will require a focus on reliability, accelerated testing, failure analysis models, clinical trials, outcome analysis, and improved understanding of the biology-biomaterial interface. This latter issue is key as seemingly minor differences in surface finish can substantially change the tissue response to an implant.

Regarding implementation strategies, the primary strategy advanced is to promote multidisciplinary research and design through mission-directed and hypothesis-driven programs. The informatics needs were articulated plainly (Eisenberger, 1996):

> "Without question, **a central resource of databases** relating to materials and devices is needed to provide uniform information on material and device performance, patient acceptance, animal test results, modes of failure, long-term survival information, and the array of additional elements needed to answer risk-benefit questions and project probabilities of success for new materials, devices, and designs. Reference materials should be made available for both research and education. These materials and the information in the database may significantly facilitate the development of improved models." (emphasis added)

The key participating government agencies charged with effecting this vision were also identified: NIH, the National Science Foundation, and NIST.

On 13 November 1998, NIST hosted a workshop to obtain a clearer assessment of the current needs for reference biomaterials with regard to standards, research, and regulatory purposes (Tesk, 2000). In addition to NIST, sponsoring organizations included NIH, FDA, and the Society for Biomaterials (SFB). Approximately 40 people attended the workshop, with 16 employed in industry. The workshop was motivated by related ongoing discussions at meetings of NIH, ASTM, and SFB. Also contributing to the timing of the workshop was a 1997 agreement among NIH, NIST, and FDA for cooperation on the development of needed reference biomaterials. The workshop established needs and priorities that strongly reflect the current status of materials selection within three biomaterials areas: orthopedic applications, cardiovascular applications, and tissue-engineered medical products.

Two high-priority reference biomaterials, composed of different forms of ultra-high molecular weight polyethylene (UHMWPE), were identified for the orthopedic industry: reference bar stock and particulate UHMWPE. The reference bar material is widely used by industry and researchers to provide a common reference for measurement comparisons and is essential for round-robin tests. The reference particulate is needed to provide a reference baseline for research into the biologic effects of particulate wear debris from artificial joints, and should provide size, size distribution, shape, and morphology typical of wear debris found around orthopedic implants that have loosened.

Representatives of the cardiovascular industry expressed support for the development of polyurethane reference materials. It was emphasized that important properties for each reference biomaterial must be clearly identified, and that a clear rationale for each proposed biomaterial must be articulated. A ready supply of reference cardiovascular biomaterials was deemed preferable to an off-the-shelf commercial product with a proprietary formulation.

With regard to tissue-engineered medical products, it was observed that this field is in an embryonic state relative to traditional biomaterials. However, a definite need for reference tissue cell-lines does exist. Due to the nascence of the field, further research is necessary to define reference cells, including the development of stable, nontransformed cell lines. It was agreed that the best approach for determining reference biomaterial needs for tissue-engineered medical products would be identified through the development of consensus standards through the activities of Division IV of the ASTM F04 Committee on Medical Devices and Surgical Materials and Devices.

Because of the need for stable, nonbiased sources for reference biomaterials, it was concluded that NIST should serve as the repository and primary distributor.

On 27 July 2000 NIST hosted a workshop to determine whether needs existed for the establishment of reference databases on the properties of biomaterials (Tesk, 2001). Among the approximately 65 workshop attendees were representatives from industry, academia, FDA, NIH, and NIST. The scope of the workshop included consideration of reference property database needs in five categories of biomaterials: orthopedic, cardiovascular, ophthalmologic, dental, and tissue-engineered. A plenary session on other issues focused specifically on database access, content, and maintenance. Also addressed was the need for non-critiqued (unevaluated) data and for reference biomaterials useful for developing data.

Generic attributes of biomaterial databases that were identified included: relevance to ISO 10993 (a set of harmonized standards that address the biological evaluation of medical devices), flexibility with regard to current literature and test data, timeliness (with frequent updating), absence of marketing hyperbole, control of data quality, and content of engineering information on usage (such as applicable shelf life). Undesirable attributes identified were: commercial charges for use of the database, administration by a regulatory agency, and data oriented to a *particular* device as opposed to a *type* of device. The database(s) developed should be available online, and should enable users to select and qualify materials rapidly. Four levels of database portals were proposed and are summarized in Table 5.

Portal	Access & User	Content	Critical review needed?
I	Public	All materials	No
II	Public	All materials	Yes, NIST-led
III	Public limited access	Reference materials	Yes, NIST
IV	FDA-Supplier-User	Specific materials	N/A to NIST

Table 5 – Biomaterial database portals

For orthopedic biomaterials, the properties deemed most useful were:
    (1) composite biomaterial properties, including:
        (a) material performance related to wear, biocompatibility, clinical and academic-type laboratory responses of biomaterials, and
        (b) properties of biomaterials according to classical descriptors;
    (2) biological response to materials:
        (a) at the cellular level, and
        (b) whole animal responses;
    (3) bulk and surface properties of materials:
        (a) pre-implantation, and
        (b) post-implantation.

It was determined that there was a need for a reference database that includes standardized test methods, properties on reference materials, and properties as derived from materials that have been processed according to those required for applications to a device.

On the subject of a cardiovascular biomaterials database, it was proposed that such a database should contain the properties of biomaterials that are relevant to specific biomedical device applications, as opposed to data according to material type and properties. Furthermore, data for device applications should be limited to realistic applications with immediate needs. The identified device-specific biomaterials and their needed properties are:

(1) chemically treated, bioprosthetic soft tissue valves
    (a) virgin mechanical properties according to classical test methods,
    (b) mechanical properties according to deformation modes,
    (c) durability for specific deformation modes, and
    (d) methods of chemical treatment and verification of cross-linking chemistry (for standardization of methods);
(2) cardiovascular device polymeric materials
    (a) biocompatibility,
    (b) platelet adhesion,
    (c) high-cycle fatigue in tension and flexure,
    (d) absorption, and
    (e) analyses of data to assess the appropriateness of time-temperature superposition methods for accelerated durability testing;
(3) endovascular stent alloys
    (a) corrosion behavior, and
    (b) shape-memory effects of virgin and low amplitude fatigue tested alloys; and
(4) arteriovenous shunts of poly(tetrafluoroethylene)
    (a) burst test results,
    (b) puncture resistance,
    (c) recovery and sealability of punctures,
    (d) biocompatibility,
    (e) platelet adhesion,
    (f) virgin mechanical properties,
    (g) high-cycle fatigue in tension and flexure, and
    (h) absorption.

Regarding an ophthalmic biomaterials database, it was determined that such a database was needed, and that it should include data on properties that would be useful for providing calibration standards. An ophthalmic biomaterials database could also be used as a stable benchmark against which other data could be evaluated. For example, currently, most intraocular lens implants are fabricated from either poly(dimethylsiloxane), poly(methyl methacrylate), or poly(hydroxyethyl methacrylate), and reference data on the properties of these implant materials are needed for benchmark and calibration purposes. The most important properties include: mechanical properties (obtained from tensile and flexural tests), optical properties (refractive index, transparency), chemical properties (surface hydrophobicity, water content), and biological behavior (interactions and safety).

The optimal dental materials database would document the composition, properties, and clinical performance of dental materials. Also identified as critical were reference methods on the characterization and processing of dental biomaterials. Database and methods priorities include: metal-implant coatings, bone graft materials (autologous and augmentation substitutes), polymeric bone fixation devices, barrier membranes, and sterilization methods.

On the question of a tissue engineered biomaterials properties database, it was proposed that nonproprietary data be obtained via a survey of key tissue engineering research organizations. The polymeric biomaterials and properties to be addressed are shown in Tables 6 and 7.

Polymer type	Examples
Natural	Alginate, collagen, chitosan, hyaluronic acid
Synthetic resorbable	Poly(ethylene glycol), poly(glycolic acid), poly(lactic acid), polyphosphazanes, poly(propylene fumarate), polytryosine
Synthetic nonresorbable	Biological mimicking pendant group substitutions

Table 6 – Tissue engineered biomaterials

Property type	Examples
Chemical/physical	Bulk chemical composition, porosity, products of degradation, degradation rate, viscosity (apparent, intrinsic), monomer and co-monomer characteristics (block length, random, alternating, etc.), molecular mass (mass average, number average, polydispersity), hydrogel properties (osmotic and pH stability, swelling, permeability, diffusion, absorption, partition), surface roughness, protein absorption
Mechanical	Elastic and flexural moduli; compressive, yield, and tensile strengths; effects of porosity and molecular mass on mechanical properties; interfacial characterizations (surface: morphology, free energy, chemical composition)

Table 7 – Tissue engineered biomaterials properties

The July 2000 workshop also identified several needed reference biomaterials, as shown in Table 8.

Category	Reference biomaterial
Orthopedic	UHMWPE (solid and particulate forms) Titanium and titanium alloys Cobalt-chromium alloys Aluminum oxide Zirconium oxide Hydroxyapatite (HA) and related calcium phosphate compounds of biological significance and use Stainless steels Poly(methyl methacrylate) Poly(lactic acid) Poly(glycolic acid) Polyfumarates Cements and glues Bioglass Coatings and surface modified materials (coatings of silver, diamond, biologics, etc.) Carbon-based composites [Note: UHMWPE Reference Material RM 8456 became available from NIST in October 2000; Standard Reference Material 2910 for HA is also available]
Cardiovascular	Polyurethanes
Ophthalmic	Poly(dimethylsiloxane) Poly(methyl methacrylate) Poly(hydroxyethyl methacrylate)
Dental	Calcium phosphate/sulfate materials Bioglass Barrier membranes Metals [Note: SRM 2910 for hydroxyapatite already exists]
Tissue-engineered	Three-dimensional reference tissue scaffolds of known porosity, interconnectivity, surface and bulk chemistry, physical and mechanical properties, and cellular reactivity

Table 8 – Needed reference biomaterials

The workshop final plenary session yielded the following conclusions:
(1) Alliances are needed among industry, government, and academia to accomplish the articulated objectives;
(2) Reference materials and databases are both needed immediately;
(3) Action is needed immediately for establishing databases from whatever methods that can be employed (for both evaluated and unevaluated data);
(4) Data from model materials is a primary need;
(5) There is a need to include both biological and material data in one source;
(6) Portals should be open as soon as possible without charge; and
(7) Tissue engineering probably needs special considerations (attention to needs).

The following roles were proposed for the participating organizations:
(1) Industry: assume leadership roles and take the lead in securing funding for reference materials (through NIH Small Business Innovation Research (SBIR) Program), provide funding to others (e.g., subcontracting of an SBIR grant), provide raw materials/final products, share existing data, conduct testing, and develop test methods;
(2) Academia: develop test methods, conduct testing, evaluate data;
(3) Government: catalyze database developments by leading in the formation of alliances, coordinate evaluated database and reference material developments, provide funding (NIH for reference materials; NIST for data), evaluate data (NIST lead with FDA counsel), design databases, and assist others in database design (NIST and FDA) and design of test methods.

As of January 2001, an alliance for ophthalmic reference data and reference materials had been formed, the beginning of an alliance for development of a reference tissue scaffold had been initiated, activities had been pursued for the development of an industry-supplied properties database, links between databases were under consideration, and an alliance for some cardiovascular synthetic reference materials continued. Further alliances were needed for the remaining biomaterials property databases and reference materials.

On 13-14 June 2001 NIST sponsored a workshop on standards for biomedical materials and devices (Anon, 2001). Workshop co-sponsors included: the Association for the Advancement of Medical Instrumentation, the American Dental Association, AdvaMed (the world's largest medical technology association representing manufacturers of medical devices, diagnostic products and medical information systems), ASTM, SFB, the National Heart, Lung, and Blood Institute, and NIH. Also cooperating were the American Institute for Medical and Biological Engineering (AIMBE) and FDA.

The primary goal of the workshop was to identify and prioritize standards needs in selected biomedical materials and devices technologies as the basis for a NIST standards strategy in those areas. A second goal of the workshop was to obtain recommendations for collaborations between NIST and other key stakeholders in the biomedical materials and devices industry to address national and international standards issues. The participants at the workshop were chosen from among a core group of idea generators and decision makers from industrial companies; organizations that shape the standards, regulatory, and research and development environment in which those companies work; and the standards community.

In general terms, workshop participants recommended that NIST contribute resources to: standards writing and standards development; committee leadership and participation; measurement and calibration methods; test method validation; databases; and Standard Reference Materials and other Reference Materials. Several workshop participants cited NIST's value as a neutral, objective party in technical matters. Also stressed by many workshop presenters was NIST's value as a source of information.

More specifically, it was proposed that NIST and AdvaMed organize and conduct workshops on the following topics:

- New biocompatibility test methods. Existing biocompatibility tests are inadequate because they fail to predict long-term adverse events. Among the key needs are predictive biocompatibility tests to assess the effects of: long term leaching of material components, materials on immune response, and carcinogenicity of materials.

- Accelerated life tests that can predict clinical performance of biomaterials. Because of the numerous devices and simulators used for device testing, it is virtually impossible to compare in a meaningful way the results from one simulator test to another in order to predict the behavior of the material in its intended application. What is needed are accelerated material tests and unifying methods of analysis that can superimpose the effects from different test and simulator-device tests and that can be applied universally (i.e., internationally).

- Methods for characterization of biomaterials and biomolecules. New test methods for assessing host response, targeted to the use and pathway for eliciting response, must be developed. Inhalation and ingestion tests are being used, for example, in cases that relate to long-term implantable materials, which dose through direct contact or through the bloodstream.

- Standardized test methods for evaluation of the biostability of materials. Tests for relevant assessment of the long-term stability of materials proposed (or used) as biomaterials do not exist. Existing tests address only short term stability and need to be reviewed as to how well they satisfy the need.

- Effects of sterilization on materials. Sterilization methods are needed for tissue engineered medical products. How sterilization by different methods may impact on long term biostability, risk assessment, lifetime performance, and biocompatibility needs to be considered. Standardized tests for assessing the effects of sterilization need to be developed.

Included in the design of the NIST Workshop on Standards for Biomedical Materials and Devices was a small data group, composed of industry and government experts experienced in data management and information technology. This group participated in the discussions of all of the workshop's breakout groups to identify the data management and information technology requirements that were discussed in those sessions. Based on these requirements, the data group formulated action plans in fifteen (15) areas for NIST to cooperate with industry in developing the needed measurements and standards. These proposed action plans are as follows:

(1) Develop a standard interface to properties of materials databases. Manufacturers of biomedical devices need access to publicly available information about the physical, chemical, and performance characteristics or properties of materials used in the manufacture of such devices. Needed is a standard way to represent different kinds of properties in a properties database so that a single software application can access multiple materials databases.

(2) Develop standardized identifiers (tags) for measurements. The biomedical materials and devices industry needs collaboration by stakeholders on standardized tags to identify physical and chemical measurements (e.g., the MatML project), and standard ways to represent different kinds of properties in a properties database so that a single software application can access multiple materials databases.

(3) Conduct a workshop on standardizing biomedical materials data registry methodology. The NIST Information Technology Laboratory has experience in standardizing data registries, and the contacts with the leaders in data registry development; thus ITL should lead in the organization of a workshop for the biomedical materials and devices industry segments.

(4) Provide technical assistance for the development of audiometric data structures. A data representative with experience in eXtensible Markup Language (XML) and data modeling is needed to work with domain experts of American National Standards Institute (ANSI) Committee S3 (Bioacoustics) WG86 to develop Audiometric Data Structures.

(5) Initiate a Technical Working Group on Ontology for Clinical Responses. The working group, in addition to recognized representatives of the biomedical materials and devices industry, should include scientists experienced in knowledge representation methodologies and software systems that draw inferences from data, and clinicians to evaluate and adopt appropriate terminology. NIST ontology specialists can assist in defining the scope and program of work for the working group, along with FDA and NIH participation.

(6) Develop data interchange standards among biomedical instruments and implant devices. Common high-level standard formats and data structures for interchanging biomedical data are needed for intra/extracorporeal communication. The Biotechnology Industry Organization (BIO) is cooperating with several major software vendors (e.g., Sun, IBM) to define standard biological data structures that can be transmitted, queried, and modified by different software systems with no loss of semantics. Interested participants are needed for the BIO effort to identify data structures and a parallel effort to represent those structures as XML documents for interchange.

(7) Develop round-robin testing protocols for assuring accuracy and precision of measurements. Generic protocols and tailored protocols for round-robin testing need to be developed to assure that appropriate numerical methods and statistical controls can be maintained throughout the round-robin testing process. Standards development organizations, biomedical materials and devices manufacturing firms, NIST materials scientists, manufacturing engineers, and statisticians, should all be involved.

(8) Establish a working group to develop patient anonymization standards. Just as traceability of test measurements to standard reference materials and test methods standards is essential, so also there is a need for the ability to trace test results back to the individual patients from which measurements and responses were derived, while maintaining confidentiality. For the effective monitoring of the clinical use of biomedical materials and devices, and for device/patient tracking over time periods, there is a need for patient anonymization standards. The working group should include clinicians from academia, government and the biotechnology industry, as well as data and IT security specialists who are working in the health area.

(9) Establish a working group to develop device/patient tracking standards. Clinicians and biomedical device manufacturers have a need for uniformly tracking these devices and patient responses over time, requiring a consensus on the types and methods of data tracking. The working group should include clinicians from academia, government and the biotechnology industry, along with data specialists working in the health area. NIST data engineers should convene the working group in order to define the scope and program of work, with cooperation from FDA and NIH clinical research specialists.

(10) Develop standards for the security of data on the measurements of biomedical materials and devices. Clinical researchers, evaluators and users of biomedical materials and devices capture and use patient healthcare information, which must be protected in accordance with national laws and regulations. There is a need for standards and measurements for protecting the integrity and confidentiality of patient data/information. Participants in the discussion should include biomedical materials and device providers, clinicians, academia, government, as well as data and information security specialists who are working in the health area. NIST can provide leadership by holding an initial meeting to coordinate standards development, conformance test development, and implementation cooperation.

(11) Identify internal NIST knowledge base and information expertise. Coordination of the NIST internal information and data expertise is needed, so that the appropriate expertise can be identified and approached for possible collaboration by organizations in the biomedical materials and devices industries. A series of workshops of NIST personnel that support information handling in all NIST laboratories and programs should be held. The goals of these workshops would be to: (1) identify and categorize all of NIST's information and data management expertise; (2) provide the relevant NIST staff with an understanding of complementary expertise in other NIST personnel; and (3) communicate these information management capabilities to the biomedical materials and devices industry to maximize the potential for Cooperative Research and Development Agreements (CRADAs) and other cooperative programs and voluntary standards activities.

(12) Conduct a workshop on ontology technology for nomenclatures, biomedical materials characterizations and device performance characterization. A fundamental difficulty in the characterization of biomedical materials and the performance of devices is the need to describe many interconnected parameters and attributes in terms of how they affect the performance of the materials and devices in different operating contexts and under different operating conditions. The semantic interconnectedness of these data items in operational contexts can be represented in computer-interpretable forms through domain ontologies. These domain ontologies can support the compatibility and consistency of the knowledge bases of each organization that supplies products in the value chain of the manufacturing processes of the specialized industry segments for different biomedical materials and devices. A NIST-sponsored workshop that will be informative for participants from the biomedical materials and devices industry is needed.

(13) Develop conformance tests for the advanced features of SQL'99. Many of the complex characterizations of materials and of the performance of devices in their operational environments need to be represented in databases in ways that can be automatically (without human examination and interpretation) interpreted by rules in other databases. Without conformance tests, implementation agreements, and protocols for interoperability testing, major errors can occur in processing data structures across different databases. Database standard developers, database systems vendors, and government agency data experts could participate in the development of conformance tests for the advanced features of SQL'99.

(14) Provide a forum and technical support for the automation of the regulatory submission/reporting processes. Manufacturers need to make submissions to various government agencies regarding the biomedical products and devices that they manufacture. Currently it is common practice to fill out the forms used by these agencies manually. To automate this process, a forum is needed where biomedical device manufacturers that prepare reports and the government agencies that receive them can meet to agree on the structure and content of reporting forms. Also necessary is participation of personnel skilled in data and process modeling and representation of data structures in some interchange format such as XML. NIST personnel with experience in data modeling and data interchange, and knowledge of existing standards, could assist in developing candidate specifications for joint approval by the affected parties.

(15) Identify coordination issues between clinical data standardization and materials and devices biomedical data requirements. As the data requirements of the biomedical materials and devices industry become better understood, it will be important to assure that no conflicts or incompatibilities are developed between clinical data standards and biomedical materials and devices data agreements. The ANSI Healthcare Informatics Standards Board (HISB) is coordinating standards development for electronic messages that include clinical data; similarly, the ANSI Medical Devices Standards Board (MDSB) coordinates standards for medical devices. NIST data scientists can become involved by identifying compatibility issues and bringing them to the appropriate standards bodies for clarification and resolution.

On September 19 to 20, 2002, the Biomaterials and Medical Implant Science (BMIS) Coordinating Committee organized a workshop to evaluate the role of the Federal government in obtaining and disseminating data gained from medical implants to ensure safer health care (Anon., 2002). The BMIS committee was formed in 1997 by Dr. Harold Varmus, then Director of NIH, and serves as a trans-agency technical group, which coordinates research programs and develops joint initiatives and workshops in biomaterials and medical implant science. The committee includes representatives from NIH, NIST, NSF, FDA, and AdvaMed.

The purpose of the September 2002 workshop was to consider the Federal government's role in providing medical implant information to ensure safer health care, and to evaluate the role for the Federal government in extracting and disseminating information gained from explanted medical implants. The goals of the workshop were threefold:

1) Define the role of the Federal government to encourage the use of explanted medical devices for research.

2) Design a structure for Federal programs to support the gathering and dissemination of data derived from medical implant retrieval.

3) Design a Federal program to promote implant retrieval for use in research intended to ensure safer health care.

Attending the workshop were 86 representatives from a wide range of backgrounds, including clinical medicine, biomedical research, information technology, law, ethics, patient advocacy, and Federal program development. Ten invited speakers discussed topics pertinent to medical implant retrieval and provided an overview of current practices in implant research and education. Following the plenary presentations, attendees addressed the goals of the workshop in four breakout sessions: Education and Information, Medical Implant Research, Non-Technical Issues, and Dimensions of Health Informatics.

The following overall workshop recommendations resulted:

1) Establish Internet-based medical implant information and data resources for patients, clinicians, researchers, designers, manufacturers, and other interested persons. These data will improve the design, fabrication, quality, and reliability of these implants and ensure enhanced safety and performance of future implants.

2) Develop standard definitions and practices for recovering implants, conducting research, evaluating outcomes, and reporting results. These standards will facilitate the creation of a reference source of aggregate data on implant device characteristics and allow electronic data exchange for long-term safety improvement and technical innovation for medical implant products.

3) Catalyze a scientific team approach to gather and disseminate a comprehensive description of implant performance and thus provide improved healthcare. The data acquired from clinical trials of a novel but critical device may demonstrate safety and efficacy over a limited time period, ranging from several months to a few years, before the device is released into commercial distribution. To improve the next generation of products, a mechanism to retrieve and evaluate more subtle aspects of device performance is also needed.

4) Educate key stakeholders about research on retrieved implants. Education about normal implant function and expected outcomes, potential adverse reactions (analogous to drug therapy), and the value of explant research all play an important role in enhancing medical device research.

5) Publish a peer-reviewed law article that clarifies the medical implant property rights of patients, manufacturers, hospitals, insurers, and other interested parties. The article will address the current state-of-the-law on ownership of both synthetic and natural retrieved implants and their use via

bequest, donation, or other contractual transfer (e.g., sale or lease) upon explantation as a result of revision surgery or death.

6) Create a central source of general information regarding the medical value, safety, lifetime, and adverse events associated with medical implants. Internet-based resources are an effective means for communicating accurate and up-to-date information in a format that is understandable to patients. This information should be derived from a standardized aggregate reference dataset that would provide consistent and dependable information.

Barriers

The barriers to progress in all of the recommendations cited above may be organized primarily into three categories: infrastructural, economic, and legal. In some cases individual barriers may effectively stymie further developments, while in other cases two or more barriers act in concert to halt progress. We shall explore each category in turn.

The principal infrastructural barrier has already been stated: the absence of established standards for testing biomaterials for all but a handful of mechanical property test methods. Recall that in the investigation of corrosion resistance, biocompatibility, and bioadhesion, the absence of standardization has led to great variations in test methods, hence the results of such tests are not comparable. A 1978 report [Galletti, 1978] identified a major roadblock to the development of materials to handle and process blood is the lack of an operational definition of blood compatibility. The scientific community had yet to agree on test and evaluation methods whereby biomechanical properties are appropriately characterized in physico-chemical terms, and whereby the blood compatibility of a material is quantitatively defined in the proper biological environment. Little progress has apparently been made in the 27 years that have elapsed since these observations were made. Despite the proliferation of data generated since then, we can hardly combine data from separate experiments if those experiments were not conducted according to established protocols.

Another infrastructural barrier is found in the multidisciplinary nature of the field. Much biomaterials research requires expertise in at least two of the following disciplines: biology, materials science/engineering, surface science, biomedical engineering, and medicine. Within medicine, many specialties draw on biomaterials: ophthalmology, orthopedics, cardiology, dermatology, surgery, and many more. Our academic institutions are largely ill equipped to handle multidisciplinary work, in both research and teaching. Federations of intellectual "silos" are more the rule than the exception in academia today. It takes at least eight years of dedicated study beyond secondary school to develop expertise (at the junior level) in any one of the fields mentioned above; the prospect of an additional 4 to 8 years of study required to develop interdisciplinary proficiency in biomaterials serves to limit the ranks of dedicated biomaterials researchers. With limited quantities of researchers, the amount of generated data that are suitable for populating biomaterials informatics is correspondingly limited.

The second category of barriers to progress is economic. Several of the panels or workshops summarized in the preceding section identified the need for a central data resource to provide a host of useful data and information in the areas of mechanical/surface properties, biological properties/response, material stability, test methods, clinical performance, etc. None of the summary panel/workshop reports indicate how to or who will fund such an undertaking. In cases where a report calls on federal agencies to lead these efforts, the agencies cited include FDA, NIH, and NIST. As above in the discussion of infrastructural barriers to progress, a combination of agencies is probably required here not only because of the multidisciplinary nature of biomaterials, but also so as to spread the cost among more partners.

Funding for implant registries is apparently difficult to obtain and sustain [Anon., 2000]. Institutions and professional societies have supported limited patient registries/databases, and manufacturers have established patient registries both voluntarily and when asked to do so by regulatory agencies. Provisioning a universal data bank – with components for tracking and adequate representation of device and patient experience over time – appears to be prohibitively expensive at this time.

The principal legal barrier to the generation of biomaterials data and informatics arises from the shortage of biomaterials as a result of litigation against biomedical device manufacturers and biomaterials suppliers [RAND, 2000]. Apparently, producers of biomaterials have felt the need to restrict the supply of their products to the makers of implantable medical devices. Both domestic and foreign companies are known to have restricted the supply of materials for implantable medical-device applications, decisions that followed in the wake of adverse litigation.

The limitations on the availability of biomaterials could have effects beyond those of limitations on available data for related informatics. Medical device firms may have to stockpile materials, diverting resources from product innovation and development to find and qualify alternative suppliers, confine their operations to offshore sites, abandon manufacturing certain products, or quit the business entirely. Academic, government, and entrepreneurial institutions may not be able to advance their research on future diagnostic and therapeutic approaches involving technologies such as tissue engineering and cell therapy and transform them into viable products, because most of these efforts require the use of biomaterials. Finally, implantable medical devices for patients may become less available.

In July 1998, Congress enacted the Biomaterials Access Assurance Act in response to this evolving situation. The act's intent was to ensure biomaterials access for device manufacturers and for those who develop implantable devices. The act affords biomaterials suppliers some shelter from liability lawsuits if they simply act as suppliers of the raw biomaterial for the medical devices and the material meets quality standards. While it is too early to tell whether the legislation is having its intended effect, a careful, fact-based examination of the evolving situation is probably warranted.

Another legal barrier in the particular case of implant retrieval and analysis arises out of uncertainties about who owns an implanted device. As with other questions about rights protected by property law, a number of parties may assert an interest in a device, and the resolution of disputes about ownership will depend-to some extent on the terms of contractual agreements among these parties. Ultimately the issue has less to do with ownership than with custody and control of potentially relevant evidence. Even if litigation is not pending, entities in possession of an explant may avoid engaging in retrieval analysis because of fear of the prospect of subsequent litigation and charges of intentional destruction of evidence. The possibility of future litigation may also discourage attempts to retrieve devices in the first place. Finally, independent researchers may hesitate to undertake implant retrieval and analysis either because litigants may subpoena their work or manufacturers may threaten product disparagement lawsuits if unflattering results are published.

In the case of implant retrieval and analysis, an additional barrier arises from religious beliefs. Among most sects, there appears to be no objection to retrieval of medical devices from living or dead persons for purposes of analysis or assessment. However, some sects strenuously oppose any mutilation of the body, either before or after death. Others make allowances for implant removal if pre- or post-mortem retrieval procedures are done in a timely manner, the wound is sutured, and the corpse is treated with respect as though it were a living patient.

Opportunities

The issues and needs surrounding biomaterials data and informatics identified above, tempered by the barriers to progress in these areas, suggest a plethora of opportunities in the field, far greater than available intellectual, infrastructural, and financial resources can provide.

With regard to the question of what types of biomaterials informatics are needed, it appears that the greater demand is for databases, regardless of subject matter, as there were no calls for expert systems, case-based reasoning systems, hypermedia, or other advanced informatics. This preference may be attributable to the relative immaturity of biomaterials as a field of research, and the paucity of standards for biomaterials property measurements. As mentioned above, this latter limitation also forestalls the development of databases with data from multiple sources, and indeed even limits straightforward comparison of such data. The application of biomaterials into biomedical devices also seems to resist classification into a collection of heuristic rules found in expert systems. Similarly, while there are numerous cases of biomaterials applications, and millions of implantations made through clinical trials and following biomedical device sales, there are no repositories of case histories that could constitute an effective case-based reasoning system – the case data are either incomplete or simply unavailable.

A pivotal development in the delivery of biomaterials data has been the rise of the Internet, or more specifically, the World Wide Web. This development is reflected in the progression of information technology cited in literature covering biomaterials data needs. The earliest such writings (approximately 20 years ago) simply cite the need for evaluated materials property data for design, with no mention of dissemination platform, the assumption undoubtedly being publication in the traditional print media, including handbooks and journals. By 1988 the biomaterials community had coalesced sufficiently to unite and call for a "National Center" to be established and develop a comprehensive database on biomaterials property data. Ten years ago the need was articulated for a central resource of databases providing uniform information on a variety of biomaterial performance data. In recent years the community consensus has included: the need for a standard interface to biomaterials property databases, standardized identifiers for measurements, and data exchange protocols, all of which suggest multiple contributors to database development, which in turn of course implies and is greatly facilitated by the Internet, or more commonly, the World Wide Web. Continuing this trend, the most recent biomaterials data delivery recommendations explicitly specify Internet-based information and data resources. With the World Wide Web considered by many the first (and often only) resort for data, the opportunity for widespread dissemination of biomaterials property and performance data is well established. Regarding the accessibility of these data, the consensus of authors who have addressed this issue is for biomaterials property data to be available as openly as possible, with respect to privacy concerns in the case of implant/explant data and intellectual property rights concerning proprietary data.

From the biomaterials science perspective, potentially pivotal new developments include: biomimetic materials (Shin, 2003), combinatorial and computational biomaterials design (Kohn, 2004), surface-modified biomaterials (Ratner, 2004a), tissue engineering (Lavik, 2004), and ultimately, regenerative medicine (Salgado, 2004). The data needs of these fields have not yet been fully articulated; however, brief consideration of the science and engineering applied in these disciplines suggest possible promising avenues of data-related work.

Biomimetics may be defined broadly as the abstraction of good design from nature. Nature has managed to build materials with broad functionality, heterogeneity and stability by using a comparatively limited number of building blocks. For example, hydroxyapatite, with composition $Ca_{10}(PO_4)_6(OH)_2$, is the principal natural material found in bone. A considerable amount of research has been conducted on the use of hydroxyapatite and other forms of calcium phosphate coupled with synthetic and other natural biomaterials to induce bone formation. Another naturally occurring calcium-based material that induces rapid bone formation is nacre, or mother-of-pearl, which constitutes the lining of many seashells. Nacre is a composite material having a mass fraction composition of more than 95 % of calcium carbonate and about 5 % protein that serves as a "mortar" to bind together a brick-like mineral structure. Nacre also has outstanding mechanical properties, comparable to those of titanium. Hence from the standpoint of mechanics alone, nacre is an attractive candidate for a bone implant, and some clinical trials have already shown success [Ni, 2003]. Both osteoinductive and mechanical properties thus make nacre a promising candidate for dental implants and bone grafting. Identification and investigation of these and other attractive biomimetic materials with accompanying relevant property data would certainly enable more widespread application of such materials.

Combinatorial and computational methodologies have been rarely used in the field of biomaterials, primarily because it has been difficult to establish appropriate computational models that can describe the complicated interactions between biomaterials and living tissue. However, computational modeling techniques have progressed sufficiently where the biomaterials discovery process may start with the creation of large virtual biomaterials libraries. With most initial work concentrated on polymeric biomaterials, virtual polymer libraries, or large collections of polymer structures, have been created using various molecular-modeling tools. The model structures are then used to derive predictions on polymer properties, thereby creating a rational means for selecting a smaller subset of virtual polymers for actual synthesis and exploration. This approach, commonly used in drug discovery, has only recently been explored as a tool in biomaterials design. In this context, quantitative structure-property relationship models enable prediction of target properties for a library of compounds, thereby accelerating and optimizing the biomaterials discovery process. Evaluation of these data for reliability and self-consistency according to established practice such as described in (Munro, 2003) would obviously improve their credibility and thereby hasten the application of these newly discovered biomaterials.

The surface chemistry and topography of biomaterials greatly influence biocompatibility and host response. A biomaterial once implanted induces an immediate biological response, termed the foreign body reaction (Anderson, 2001), which occurs whether the biomaterial is ceramic, metallic, or polymeric. In brief, a biomaterial elicits nonspecific protein absorption immediately upon implantation. Chronic inflammation at the biomaterial interface ensues, and ultimately the immune system walls off the device by a collagenous fibrous tissue that is typically 50 µm to 200 µm thick. This fibrous capsule can lead to clinical complications at the biomaterial/tissue interface, such as capsular contracture of breast implants, insulating barriers around electrodes, scarring around heart valves, fibrous layers surrounding vascular grafts, opacification of intraocular lenses, and even inflammation seen with some contact lenses. A considerable amount of research explores biomaterial surfaces that control protein absorption. Another important biomaterial surface parameter that influences host response is implant microarchitecture. Nonporous implants result in densely packed, well-organized fibrous capsules, whereas certain porous implants lead to a less dense, more open and disorganized fibrous capsule. Porous membranes, with pores between 5 µm and 15 µm, result in significantly increased vascularization adjacent to the implant and within the fibrous capsule as compared with smooth surfaces, and regardless of surface chemistry. This increased vascularization leads to enhanced diffusion of small molecules across the membrane, and hence improves implant biocompatibility. The importance of improved understanding of biomaterial surfaces cannot be overstated. A compilation, review, and/or evaluation of available biomaterial surface properties would greatly assist biomedical researchers in modifying or engineering surfaces to overcome nonspecific protein absorption *in vivo* and minimize the foreign body reaction.

The basic premise of tissue engineering is to combine living cells with a biomaterial under conditions that lead to tissue growth. The nature of the biomaterial and its physical and chemical properties are critical to creating the desired conditions for tissue formation. A host of different biomaterials have been used in tissue engineering. Ceramics and metals have been used primarily in orthopedic and dental applications (Hench, 1998; Puleo, 1999). The mechanical properties of metals and ceramics along with the bioactivity of certain ceramics, including hydroxyapatite and Bioglass, have made them very successful in hard tissue applications such as bones and teeth; however, they are less suitable for soft tissues. Polymeric biomaterials more closely match the chemical and mechanical properties of a greater variety of biological tissues (Seal, 2001). Tissue engineering advances will rest upon advances in biodegradable polymers, rapid prototyping, drug delivery, stem cell methodologies, and biomimetic strategies for recreating extracellular, matrix-like biomimetic materials. The biomaterials data needs in tissue engineering have been articulated in (Tesk, 2001). The principal objective identified is to develop a tissue engineered materials properties database, which would include chemical, physical, and mechanical characterizations of natural, synthetic resorbable, and synthetic nonresorbable polymer biomaterials. The scope of this database could be broadened to include ceramic and metallic materials used in tissue engineering. In addition to such a database, new tissue engineered reference materials, and advances in cell culture, gene delivery, cell and tissue storage, sterilization, and surgery will be needed to fully realize the potential of tissue engineering.

The roles for the key organizations and individuals who can best exploit the opportunities described above are critical for success in any biomaterials property data effort. Academic researchers should continue advancing the biomaterial research frontier, expanding the corpus of biomaterials science and technology, and training future generations of biomedical scientists and engineers. More specifically, and with respect to biomaterials data, academia should develop test methods, conduct experiments that yield biomaterial property data, and evaluate these data. Biomaterial and medical societies should continue to publish research findings and data, provide forums for presentation of the latest results, and lead in the formation of alliances among all interested parties. Biomaterial suppliers and biomedical device manufacturers should respectively provide raw materials and final product, share existing data, lead standardization efforts, develop test methods, and conduct testing. Government agencies should continue to fund biomaterials research, reference materials and data (NIH); and also facilitate standards development, evaluate data, design databases, and assist others in design of test methods and database design (NIST, FDA). Examples of specific data-related tasks include reviews of literature, assessments and critiques of literature data, design of databases, accrual of data, and assemblage and maintenance of databases. With respect to reference biomaterials, parallel efforts include fabrication or procurement of materials, test design and testing of reference materials for properties, and statistical analyses of data.

Finally, regarding communication of these opportunities in biomaterials data, it is probably not yet timely to conduct another forum, panel, or workshop on this subject. The last known relevant event, the Biomaterials and Medical Implant Science Coordinating Committee Workshop (Anon., 2002), occurred less than three years ago; more importantly, most of the recommendations of this workshop and prior related events remain valid yet unfulfilled. The need for reliable biomaterials property data continues to increase along with advances in research and the growth of the biomedical device industry. Such data are generated prodigiously and published continuously, but available compendia have been found lacking. For example, the only online non-proprietary source of biomaterials properties data (O'Brien, 1997b) greatly needs expansion of its scope (the current emphasis is on dental materials) and updating (over eight years have elapsed since the last update).

Many consider regenerative medicine, which will provide for *in vivo* regeneration of whole organs and tissues, the grail of biomedical science and technology whose realization will ultimately supplant tissue engineering and render conventional biomaterials obsolete. Technologies important to making regenerative medicine a reality include advances in stem cell biology, gene delivery, and the controlled release of bioactive substances. Successful *in vivo* regeneration of whole organs and tissues will require the combined and dedicated expertise of many fields, including: chemistry, chemical engineering, pharmaceutics, physics, materials science and engineering, and the biological disciplines – biochemistry, biophysics, genetic engineering, molecular and cell biology, physiology, biomedical engineering, and of course, medicine. While regenerative medicine may preclude the need for synthetic materials in the body, many applications will continue to require synthetics, and the need for compatible biomaterials and reliable performance and property data will continue well through the 21st century.

References

Anderson, J.M., Biological responses to materials. *Annual Review of Materials Research*, Vol. 31, pp. 81-110, 2001.

Anon., *Improving Medical Implant Performance Through Retrieval Information: Challenges and Opportunities*. National Institutes of Health, NIH Technology Assessment Conference Summary, January 10-12, 2000. Available online at: http://www.ncbi.nlm.nih.gov/books.

Anon., *Materials Science and Engineering for the 1990s: Maintaining Competitiveness in the Age of Materials*. Washington, DC: National Academy Press, 1989.

Anon., *Medical Implant Information, Performance, and Policies Workshop Final Report*, Rockville, MD, September 19-20, 2002, 27 pp., http://www.nbib1.nih.gov/events/BMIS/BMIS2002.htm.

Anon., *Workshop on Standards for Biomedical Materials and Devices, NISTIR 6791*. Gaithersburg, MD: National Institute of Standards and Technology, 2001.

Barenberg, S.A., Abridged report of the committee to survey the needs and opportunities for the biomaterials industry. *Journal of Biomedical Materials Research*, Vol. 22, pp. 1267-1291, 1988.

Barenberg, S.A., Report of the Committee to Survey Needs and Opportunities for the Biomaterials Industry. *MRS Bulletin*, Vol. 16, pp. 26-32, September 1991.

Berman, H. M., Olson, W. K., Beveridge, D. L., Westbrook, J., Gelbin, A., Demeny, T., Hsieh, S.-H., Srinivasan, A. R., and Schneider, B.: The Nucleic Acid Database: A Comprehensive Relational Database of Three-Dimensional Structures of Nucleic Acids. *Biophysical. Journal*, Vol. 63, pp. 751-759, 1992. Maintained online at: http://ndbserver.rutgers.edu/.

Berman, H.M., Westbrook, J., Feng, Z., Gilliland, G., Bhat, T.N., Weissig, H., Shindyalov, I.N., Bourne, P.E.: The Protein Data Bank. *Nucleic Acids Research*, 28 pp. 235-242, 2000. Maintained online at: http://www.rcsb.org/pdb/.

Black, J., and Hastings, G., eds., *Handbook of Biomaterials Properties*. 616 pp., Chapman and Hall, 1998.

Castner, D.G., and Ratner, B.D., Biomedical surface science: Foundations to frontiers. *Surface Science*, Vol. 500, pp. 28-60, 2002.

Cooper, S.L., Visser, S.A., Hergenrother, R.W., and Lamba, N.M.K.: Polymers. Chapter 2.2, pp. 67-79 of Ratner, B.D., Hoffman, A.S., Schoen, F.J., and Lemons, J.E., eds., *Biomaterials Science: an Introduction to Materials in Medicine, 2nd Edition*. Academic Press, San Diego, CA, 2004.

Donachie, M., Biomaterials. In: *ASM Metals Handbook, Desk Edition, 2nd ed.*, pp. 702-709, Materials Park, OH: ASM International, 1998.

Eisenberger, P., Rekow, D., Jelinski, L.W., Marlow, D.E., McKinlay, S.M., Meyer, A.E., Potvin, A.R., Ratner, B.D., Watson, J.T., Braveman, N., Cassatt, J., Didisheim, P., Holloway, C., and Panagis, J.S., Biomaterials and medical implant science: Present and future perspectives: A summary report. *Journal of Biomedical Materials Research*, Vol. 32, pp. 143-147, 1996.

Engelberg, I., and Kohn, J., Physico-mechanical properties of degradable polymers used in medical applications: a comparative study. *Biomaterials*, Vol. 12, pp. 292-304, April 1991.

Galletti, P.M., Brash, J.L., Keller, K.H., La Farge, G., Mason, R.G., Pierce, W.S., and Reynolds, J.A., Report of the Task Force on Biomaterials to the Cardiology Advisory Committee of the NHLBI. *Cardiovascular Diseases, Bulletin of the Texas Heart Institute*, Vol. 5, No. 3, pp. 293-314, September 1978.

Gilliland, G.L., Tung, M., Blakeslee, D.M. and Ladner, J. 1994. The Biological Macromolecule Crystallization Database, Version 3.0: New Features, Data, and the NASA Archive for Protein Crystal Growth Data. *Acta Crystallogr.* D50 408-413. Maintained online at: http://wwwbmcd.nist.gov:8080/bmcd/bmcd.html.

Hench, L.L., Bioactive materials: The potential for tissue regeneration. *Journal of Biomedical Materials Research*, Vol. 41, No. 4, pp. 511-518, 1998.

Kohn, J., New approaches to biomaterials design. *Nature Materials*, Vol. 3, pp. 745-747, November 2004.

Lavik, E., and Langer, R., Tissue engineering: current state and perspectives. *Applied Microbiology and Biotechnology*, Vol. 65, pp. 1-8, 2004.

Migliaresi, C., and Alexander, H., Composites. Chapter 2.12, pp. 181-197 of Ratner, B.D., Hoffman, A.S., Schoen, F.J., and Lemons, J.E., eds., *Biomaterials Science: an Introduction to Materials in Medicine, 2nd Edition*. Academic Press, San Diego, CA, 2004.

Mueller, E.P., and Barenberg, E.P., Biomaterials in an Emerging National Materials Science Agenda. *MRS Bulletin*, Vol. 16, pp. 86-87, September 1991.

Munro, R.G., *Data Evaluation Theory and Practice for Materials Properties*. NIST Recommended Practice Guide Special Publication 960-11, Washington: U.S. Government Printing Office, 2003.

National Research Council, *Guide for the Care and Use of Laboratory Animals*, National Academy Press, Washington, DC, 1996.

Ni, M., and Ratner, B.D., Nacre surface transformation to hydroxyapatite in a phosphate buffer solution. *Biomaterials*, Vol. 24, pp. 4323-4331.

O'Brien, W.J., ed., *Dental Materials and Their Selection*, 2nd ed., Quintessence Publishing, Inc., 1997. (O'Brien, 1997a).

O'Brien, W.J., University of Michigan Biomaterials Properties Database. Maintained online at: http://www.lib.umich.edu/dentlib/Dental_tables/intro.html, 1997. (O'Brien, 1997b).

Park, J.B., *Biomaterials*. Chapter IV of *The Biomedical Engineering Handbook*, Bronzino, J.D., Ed.-in-Chief, CRC Press, 1995.

Park, J.B., and Lakes, R.S., *Biomaterials: an Introduction*. Second edition. Plenum Press, New York, NY, 1992.

Puleo, D.A., and Nanci, A., Understanding and controlling the bone-implant interface. *Biomaterials*, Vol. 20, pp. 2311-2321, 1999.

RAND, Biomaterials Availability: Potential Effects on Medical Innovation and Health Care. *RAND Issue Paper IP-194*, January 2000. Available online at: http://www.rand.org/publications/IP/IP194/IP194.pdf.

Ratner, B.D., and Bryant, S.J., Biomaterials: Where We Have Been and Where We Are Going. *Annual Reviews of Biomedical Engineering*, Vol. 6, pp. 41-75, 2004. (Ratner, 2004a).

Ratner, B.D., Hoffman, A.S., Schoen, F.J., and Lemons, J.E., eds., *Biomaterials Science: an Introduction to Materials in Medicine.* 484 pp. Academic Press, San Diego, CA, 1996.

Ratner, B.D., Hoffman, A.S., Schoen, F.J., and Lemons, J.E., eds., *Biomaterials Science: an Introduction to Materials in Medicine, 2nd Edition.* 851 pp. Academic Press, San Diego, CA, 2004. (Ratner, 2004b).

Rawlings, R.D., Bioactive Glasses and Glass-Ceramics. *Clinical Materials*, Vol. 14, pp. 155-179, 1993.

Salgado, A.J., Coutinho, O.P., and Reis, R.L., Bone Tissue Engineering: State of the Art and Future Trends. *Macromolecular Bioscience*, Vol. 4, pp. 743-765, 2004.

Seal, B.L., Otero, T.C., and Panitch, A., Polymeric biomaterials for tissue and organ regeneration. *Materials Science and Engineering R*, Vol. 34, pp. 147-230, 2001.

Shin, H., Jo, S., and Mikos, A.G., Biomimetic materials for tissue engineering. *Biomaterials*, Vol. 24, pp. 4353-4364, 2003.

Tesk, J.A., NIST workshop on needs for reference biomaterials. *Journal of Biomedical Materials Research*, Vol. 51, pp. 155-156, 2000.

Tesk, J.A., NIST Workshop on Reference Data for the Properties of Biomaterials. *Journal of Biomedical Materials Research (Applied Biomaterials)*, Vol. 58, pp. 463-466, 2001.

Williams, D.F., *Definitions in Biomaterials. Proceedings of a Consensus Conference of the European Society for Biomaterials*, Chester, England, March 3-5, 1986, Vol. 4, New York: Elsevier, 1987.

Appendices

Abbreviations and acronyms

AAMI	Association for the Advancement of Medical Instrumentation
AAOS	American Academy of Orthopaedic Surgeons
ACC	American College of Cardiology
ADA	American Dental Association
AdvaMed	Advanced Medical Technology Association
AES	Auger electron spectroscopy
AFM	Atomic force microscopy
AIMBE	American Institute for Medical and Biological Engineering
AMA	American Medical Association
ANSI	American National Standards Institute
ASTM	American Society for Testing and Materials
ATR	Attenuated total reflectance
BIO	Biotechnology Industry Organization
BMCD	Biological Macromolecule Crystallization Database
BMIS	Biomaterials and Medical Implant Science
CARB	Center for Advanced Research in Biotechnology
CRADA	Cooperative Research and Development Agreement
DOE	Department of Energy
DNA	Deoxyribonucleic acid
ePTFE	Expanded polytetrafluoroethylene
ESCA	Electron spectroscopy for chemical analysis
FDA	Food and Drug Administration
FTIR	Fourier transform infrared
HA	Hydroxyapatite
HISB	[ANSI] Healthcare Informatics Standards Board
ISO	International Organization for Standardization
MatML	Materials markup language
MDSB	[ANSI] Medical Devices Standards Board
NAE	National Academy of Engineering
NAS	National Academy of Sciences
NASA	National Aeronautics and Space Administration
NCI	National Cancer Institute
NCRR	National Center for Research Resources
NDB	Nucleic acid database
NHLBI	National Heart, Lung, and Blood Institute
NIBIB	National Institute of Biomedical Imaging and Bioengineering
NIGMS	National Institute of General Medical Sciences
NIH	National Institutes of Health
NINDS	National Institute of Neurological Disorders and Stroke
NIST	National Institute of Standards and Technology
NLM	National Library of Medicine
NRC	National Research Council
NSF	National Science Foundation
ORS	Orthopedic Research Society
PDB	Protein data bank
PDO	Poly(p-dioxanone)
PE	Polyethylene
PET	Poly(ethylene terephthalate)
PGA	Poly(glycolic acid)

PLA	Poly(lactic acid)
PMM	Poly(methyl methacrylate)
PTFE	Polytetrafluoroethylene
PTMC	Poly(trimethylene carbonate)
PUR	Polyurethane
PVC	Poly(vinyl chloride)
RCSB	Research Collaboratory for Structural Bioinformatics
RM	Reference material
RNA	Ribonucleic acid
SBIR	Small Business Innovation Research
SEM	Scanning electron microscopy
SFB	Society for Biomaterials
SIMS	Secondary ion mass spectrometry
SQL	Structured query language
SRM	Standard reference material
SS	Stainless steel
STM	Scanning tunneling microscopy
SVS	Society for Vascular Surgery
TCP	Tricalcium phosphate
UHMWPE	Ultra-high-molecular-weight polyethylene
WWW	World Wide Web
XML	Extensible markup language

Glossary of Terms

The following definitions are largely drawn from: (Dee, 2002), (Ramakrishna, 2001), and (Williams, 1987):

Term	Definition
Acetabulum	The socket portion of the hip joint.
Allograft	A graft taken from another individual of the same species as the recipient. Also called 'homograft'.
Alveolar bone	The bone structure that supports and surrounds the roots of teeth.
Amalgam	An alloy of two or more metals, one of which is mercury.
Anastomosis	Interconnection between two blood vessels.
Aneurysm	Abnormal dilatation of bulging of a segment of a blood vessel.
Ankylosis	Fixation of a joint; in dentistry, the rigid fixation of the tooth to the alveolar bone and ossification of the periodontal membrane.
Anterior	Direction referring to the front side of the body.
Apical	Near the apex or extremity of a conical structure, such as the tip of the root of a tooth.
Arthritis	Inflammation of joints.
Arthrodesis	Fusion or fixation of a joint.
Arthroplasty	Surgical repair of a joint.
Articular cartilage	The cartilage at the ends of bones in joints which serve as the articulating, bearing surface.
Artificial organ	A medical device that replaces, in part or in whole, the function of one of the organs of the body.
Atrophy	Wasting away of tissues or organs.
Autograft	A graft taken from a source in the individual who receives it; that is, the donor and recipient are the same person.
Bioactive material	A material which has been designed to induce specific biological activity, often forming a bond with living tissue.
Bioadhesion	The adhesion of cells and/or tissue to the surface of a material.
Bioattachment	The fastening of cells and/or tissue to the surface of a material, including mechanical interlocking.
Biocompatibility	The ability of a material to perform with an appropriate host response in a specific application.
Biodegradable	Refers to materials that degrade (by hydrolytic breakdown) in the body while they are being replaced by regenerating natural tissue; the chemical by-products of the degrading materials are absorbed and released via metabolic processes of the body.
Bioglass	Surface-active glass compositions that have been shown to bond to tissue. Registered trademark of the University of Florida.
Bioinert	Refers to a material that retains its structure in the body and does not induce any immunologic host reactions.
Biological material	A material produced by a biological system.
Biomaterial	A nonviable material used in a medical device, intended to interact with biological systems.
Biomimetics	An interdisciplinary field in materials science, engineering, and biology, studying the use of biological principles for synthesis or fabrication of materials inspired by nature.
Bioprosthesis	An implantable prosthesis that consists totally or substantially of nonviable, treated, donor tissue.
Bioresorption	The process of removal by cellular activity and/or dissolution of a material in a biological environment.
Bone cement	A biomaterial used to secure a firm fixation of joint prostheses, such as hip

	and knee joints. It is primarily made of polymethyl methacrylate powder and monomer methyl methacrylate liquid.
Callus	The hard substance that is formed around a bone fracture during healing. It is usually replaced with compact bone.
Cancellous bone	The reticular or spongy tissue of bone where spicules or trabeculae form the interconnecting latticework that is surrounded by connective tissue or bone marrow.
Catheter	An instrument (tube) for gaining access to a draining or sampling fluids in the body.
Cochlear implant	A type of surgically implanted hearing aid used to treat sensorineural hearing loss.
Collagen	The supporting protein from which the fibers of connective tissues are formed.
Compression plate	Bone plate designed to give compression on the fracture site of a broken bone for fast healing.
Condylar prostheses	Artificial knee joints.
Connective tissue	The matrix-continuous tissue which binds together and is the support of all of the structures of the body.
Cortical bone	The compact hard bone with osteons.
Crown	The part of tooth that is exposed above the gum line or covered with enamel. Largely made of hydroxyapatite mineral.
Dacron	Polyethylene terephthalate polyester that is made into fibers, a product of Dupont Co., USA. The same polymer made into film is called Mylar.
Dental caries	Tooth decay caused by acid-forming microorganisms.
Dental restoration	Another name for dental fillings.
Dentine	The main substance of the tooth, with properties and composition similar to bone.
Dermatitis	Inflammation of the skin.
Dura mater	The dense, tough connective tissue over the surface of the brain.
Elastin	The elastic fibrous mucoprotein in connective tissue.
Enamel	A hard, white substance that covers the dentine of the crown of a tooth; enamel is the hardest substance in the body.
Endosseous	In the bone, referring to dental implants fixed to the jaw bone.
Endosteal	Related to the membrane lining the inside of the bone cavities.
Explant	An implant that has been surgically removed.
Extracorporeal	Outside the body.
Femur	The thigh bone, the bone of the upper leg.
Fibrinogen	Large plasma protein that plays a critical role in blood clotting as well as several other physiological and pathological processes.
Fixation devices	Implants used during bone-fracture repair to immobilize the fracture.
Fracture plate	Plate used to fix broken bones by open (surgical) reduction. It is fixed to the bone by using screws.
Gingiva	The gum tissue; the dense fibrous tissue overlying the alveolar bone in the mouth and surrounding the necks of teeth.
Graft	A piece of viable tissue or collection of viable cells transferred from a donor site to a recipient site for the purpose of reconstruction of the recipient site.
Hard tissue	The general term for calcified structures in the body, such as bone.
Heparin	A substance (mucopolysaccharide acid) found in various body tissues that prevents the clotting of blood.
Herniated disk	Rupture of the central portion, or nucleus, of the disk through the disk wall and into the spinal canal. Also called a slipped disk.
Heterograft	A graft from one species to another. Also called xenograft.
Host response	The reaction of a living system to the presence of a material.
Hyaline cartilage	Cartilage with a frosted glassy appearance.

Hybrid artificial organ	An artificial organ that is a combination of viable cells and one or more biomaterials.
Hydrogel	Highly hydrated (over 30 % by weight) polymer gel. Acrylamide and poly-HEMA (hydroxyethymethacrylate) are two common hydrogels.
Hydroxyapatite	Mineral component of bone and teeth. A calcium phosphate, with composition $Ca_{10}(PO_4)_6(OH)_2$.
Ilizarov technique	A technique used most often in reconstructive settings to lengthen limbs, transport bone segments, and correct angular deformities.
Implant	A medical device made from one or more biomaterials that is intentionally placed within the body, either totally or partially buried beneath an epithelial surface.
Intervertebral disc	A flat, circular platelike structure of cartilage that serves as a cushion, or shock absorber, between the vertebrae.
Intima	Inner lining of a blood vessel.
Intramedullary rod or nail	An orthopedic rod or nail inserted into the intramedullary marrow cavity of the bone to promote healing of long bone fractures.
Intraosseous implant	An implant inserted into the bone.
In vitro	Simulated in vivo condition in the laboratory.
In vivo	Inside the living body.
Kirschener wire	Metal surgical wires.
Kyphosis	Abnormally increased convexity in the curvature of the lumbar spine.
Ligament	A sheet or band of fibrous connective tissue that join bone to bone, offering support to the joint.
Long bones	Bones that are longer than they are wide with distinctive shaped ends, such as the femur.
Lordosis	Abnormally increased concavity in the curvature of the lumbar spine.
LTI carbon	Low-temperature isotropic carbon.
Lumen	The space within a tubular structure.
Mandibular bone	Lower jaw of the mouth.
Maxillary bone	Upper jaw of the mouth.
Medical device	An instrument, apparatus, implement, machine, contrivance, in vitro reagent, or other similar or related article, including any component, part or accessory, which is intended for use in the diagnosis of disease or other conditions, or in the cure, mitigation, treatment or prevention of disease in man.
Medullary cavity	The marrow cavity inside the long bones.
Myocardium	The muscular tissue of the heart.
Necrosis	Death of tissues.
Nonunion	A bone fracture that does not join.
Occlusion	Becoming close together; in dentistry, bringing the teeth together as during biting and chewing.
Organ	Two or more tissues combined to form a larger functional unit.
Orthopedics	The medical field concerned with the skeletal system.
Osseointegration	Direct biochemical bonding between a non-natural substance and bony tissue.
Ossicles	The small bones of the middle ear which transmit sound from the ear drum to the body.
Osteoarthritis	A degenerative joint disease, characterized by softening of the articular ends of bones and thickening of joints, sometimes resulting in partial ankylosis.
Osteopenia	Loss of bone mass due to failure of osteoid synthesis.
Osteoporosis	The abnormal reduction of the density and increase in porosity of bone due to demineralization, commonly seen in the elderly.
Osteotomy	Cutting of bone to correct a deformity.
Oxygenator	An apparatus by which oxygen is introduced into blood during circulation

	outside the body, as during open-heart surgery.
Percutaneous device	A medical device that passes through the skin, remaining in that position for a significant length of time.
Periodontal ligament	Periodontium; the connective tissue (ligament) joining the tooth to the alveolar bone.
Permucosal device	A medical device that passes through a mucosal surface, remaining in that position for a significant length of time.
Plasticizer	Substance made of small molecules, mixed with amorphous polymers to make the chains slide more easily past each other, making the polymer less rigid.
Posterior	Direction referring to the back side of the body.
Proplast	A composite material made of fibrous PTFE and carbon. It is usually porous and has low modulus and low strength.
Prosthesis	A device that replaces a limb, organ or tissue of the body.
Proximal	Nearest the trunk or point of origin.
Pyrolitic carbon	Isotropic carbon coated onto a substrate in a fluidized bed.
Regeneration	The renewal of a tissue or organ at the completion of healing.
Remodeling/ Maintenance/ Turnover	The process by which extracellular matrix is replaced in a process of degradation followed by synthesis.
Repair	The formation of a scar at a site of injury at the completion of healing.
Resorption	Dissolution or removal of a substance.
Rheumatoid arthritis	Chronic and progressive inflammation of the connective tissue of joints, leading to deformation and disability.
Scoliosis	An abnormal lateral (sideward) curvature of a portion of the spine.
Silastic	Medical grade silicone rubber, Dow Corning Corporation.
Silica	The ceramic silicon oxide, SiO_2.
Spondylosis	Any of various degenerative diseases of the spine.
Spondylolisthesis	Forward bending of the body at one of the lower vertebrae.
Stapes	One of the ossicles of the middle ear.
Stenosis	A narrowing or constriction of the diameter of a bodily passage or orifice.
Stress-shield effect	Prolonged reduction of stress on a bone which may result in porotic bone (osteoporosis), which may weaken it. This process can be reversed if the natural state of stress can be restored to its original state.
Subcutaneous	Beneath the skin.
Subperiosteal	Underneath the periosteum.
Suture	Material used in closing a wound with stitches.
Synovial fluid	The clear viscous fluid that lubricates the surfaces of joints and tendons, secreted by the synovial membrane.
Tendon	A band or cord of fibrous tissue.
THR	Total hip replacement.
Thromboembolism	An obstruction in the circulatory system caused by a dislodged thrombus.
Thrombogenicity	The property of a material which induces and/or promotes the formation of a thrombus.
Thrombosis	Formation of a thrombus, a blood clot.
Thrombus	A fibrinous blood clot.
Tissue	An aggregation of similarly specialized cells united in the performance of a particular function. Cells serving the same general function and having the same extracellular matrix.
Tissue engineering	Tissue repair initiated *in vitro* on cellularly seeded scaffolds and then transplanted to the recipient.
Tissue regeneration	*In situ* repair of host tissue.
TKR	Total knee replacement.
Transplant	A complete structure, such as an organ, that is transferred from a site in a donor to a site in a recipient for the purpose of reconstruction of the recipient

	site.
Ureter	The tube that conducts urine from the kidney to the bladder.
Urethra	The canal leading from the bladder to the outside for discharging urine.
Vitallium	A Co-Cr alloy, Howmedica Inc.
Vitreous carbon	A term generally applied to isotropic carbon with very small crystallites.
Wolff's law	The principle relating the internal structure and architecture of bone to external mechanical stimuli. Remodeling of bone takes place in response to mechanical stimulation so that the new structure becomes suitably adapted to the load.
Xenograft	A graft taken from an individual of a different species to the recipient. Also called heterograft.

Web Resources of Special Interest

Andrade, J., Biomaterials I: Past, Present and Future. http://summit.whitaker.org/white/biomat1.pdf, Arlington, VA: The Whitaker Foundation, December 2000.

Anon., AdvaMed – Trade association representing medical device manufacturers, makers of medical equipment, medical software and information systems.
http://www.advamed.org/.

Anon., Biomaterials – Densities of Biomaterials and Some Other Related Materials.
http://www.azom.com/details.asp?ArticleID=1413, 2004.

Anon., Biomat.net. Online network providing an interactive source of information aimed at providing organized and meaningful biomaterials communication.
http://www.biomat.net/.

Anon., Biomedical Materials. *Chemistry for Health*, (briefing paper #2),
http://www.rsc.org/pdf/publicaf/chbp2.pdf, London, Royal Society of Chemistry, March 1999.

Anon., Calcium Phosphate Biomaterials – Solubility of Calcium Phosphates.
http://www.azom.com/details.asp?ArticleID=2140, 2004.

Anon., Cobalt-Chrome Stents Receive FDA Approval, http://www.azom.com/details.asp?ArticleID=2144, 2004.

Anon., Data Sheet No. 14: Titanium for Medical Applications, Titanium Information Group,
http://www.titaniuminfogroup.co.uk/i/pdfs/data14.pdf, 2001.

Anon., Gold – Applications and Developments in the Electronics, Biomaterials and Catalysis. *Materials World*, Vol. 11, No. 2, pp. 12-14, February 2003. See also
http://www.azom.com/details.asp?ArticleID=1899, 2004.

Anon., *Improving Medical Implant Performance Through Retrieval Information: Challenges and Opportunities*. National Institutes of Health, NIH Technology Assessment Conference Summary, January 10-12, 2000. Available online at: http://www.ncbi.nlm.nih.gov/books.

Anon., Materials Selection for Total Hip Replacement. http://www.materials.qmul.ac.uk/casestud/implants, London, Department of Materials, Queen Mary, University of London, 2004.

Anon., *Medical Implant Information, Performance, and Policies Workshop Final Report*, Rockville, MD, September 19-20, 2002, 27 pp., http://www.nbib1.nih.gov/events/BMIS/BMIS2002.htm.

Anon., Orthopaedic Biomaterials Market Review. http://www.azom.com/details.asp?ArticleID=1361, 2004.

Anon., Society for Biomaterials – Professional society that promotes advances in all phases of biomaterials research and development. http://www.biomaterials.org/.

Anon., Sodium Citrate Modified Calcium Phosphate Cement for Bone Repair Applications. *Materials World*, Vol. 12, No. 3, p. 12, March 2004. See also: http://www.azom.com/details.asp?ArticleID=2528.

Anon., Supplier Data – Polyhydroxybutyrate – (PHB) Biopolymer (Goodfellow),
http://www.azom.com/details.asp?ArticleID=1881, 2004.

Anon., Titanium Alloys – Ti6Al7Nb Properties and Applications, http://www.azom.com/details.asp?ArticleID=2064, 2004.

Anon., Titanium and Titanium Alloys as Biomaterials, http://www.azom.com/Details.asp?ArticleID=1520, 2004.

Anon., UK Biomaterials Portal – U.K. industry links and resources. http://www.biomaterials.org.uk/.

ASTM Biomaterials Standards – all are from: *Annual Book of ASTM Standards, Vol. 13.01*; West Conshohocken, PA: American Society for Testing and Materials, 2000. For information on Committee F04 on Medical and Surgical Materials and Devices, see http://www.astm.org/cgi-bin/SoftCart.exe/COMMIT/COMMITTEE/F04.htm?L+mystore+wbor6766+1109882759.

Berman, H. M., Olson, W. K., Beveridge, D. L., Westbrook, J., Gelbin, A., Demeny, T., Hsieh, S.-H., Srinivasan, A. R., and Schneider, B.: The Nucleic Acid Database: A Comprehensive Relational Database of Three-Dimensional Structures of Nucleic Acids. *Biophysical Journal*, Vol. 63, pp. 751-759, 1992. Maintained online at: http://ndbserver.rutgers.edu/.

Berman, H.M, Westbrook, J., Feng, Z., Gilliland, G., Bhat, T.N., Weissig, H., Shindyalov, I.N., and Bourne, P.E.: The Protein Data Bank. *Nucleic Acids Research*, 28 pp. 235-242, 2000. Maintained online at: http://www.rcsb.org/pdb/.

Binner, J., and Sambrook, R., Break out the bubbly – new ceramic foams. *Materials World*, Vol. 10, No. 2, pp. 13-15, February 2002. See also: http://www.azom.com/details.asp?ArticleID=1869.

Borgersen, S., Safety and Innovation in Biomedical Device Design: the Increasing Role of Simulation. *The Journal of Virtual Product Development*, Vol. 2, Spring 2004, http://www.coe.org/newsnet/sept04/.

Burg, T., and Standard, O., *Materials for Biomedical Engineering*, Student Notes, School of Materials Science and Engineering, University of New South Wales, http://www.materials.unsw.edu.au/news/biomed-s.pdf, 2001.

Burg, T., and Standard, O., *Materials for Biomedical Engineering*, Teacher Reference, School of Materials Science and Engineering, University of New South Wales, http://www.materials.unsw.edu.au/news/biomed-t.pdf, 2001.

Cordingley, R., Kohan, L., Ben-Nissan, B., and Pezzotti, G., Alumina and Zirconia Bioceramics in Orthopaedic Applications. *Journal of the Australasian Ceramic Society*, Vol. 39, No. 1, pp. 20-28, 2003. See also: http://www.azom.com/Details.asp?ArticleID=2160, http://www.azom.com/Details.asp?ArticleID=2161.

Eisenbarth, E., and Morlock, M., Biomaterials. http://www.tu.harburg.de/bim/lecture/biomaterials/biomaterials.2004.02.pdf.

Elsevier, *Biomaterials*. Online version of print journal. http://www.sciencedirect.com/science/journal/01429612.

Gilliland, G.L., Tung, M., Blakeslee, D.M. and Ladner, J. 1994. The Biological Macromolecule Crystallization Database, Version 3.0: New Features, Data, and the NASA Archive for Protein Crystal Growth Data. *Acta Crystallogr.* D50 408-413. Maintained online at http://wwwbmcd.nist.gov:8080/bmcd/bmcd.html.

Gross, K., Bioceramics – An Overview Including Calcium Phosphates, Hydroxyapatite, Alumina, Zirconia, and Pyrolytic Carbon. http://www.azom.com/details.asp?ArticleID=1743, 2004.

Heness, G., and Ben-Nissan, B., Innovative Bioceramics. *Materials Forum*, Vol. 27, pp. 104-114, 2004. See also: http://www.azom.com/Details.asp?ArticleID=2632, http://www.azom.com/Details.asp?ArticleID=2630, http://www.azom.com/Details.asp?ArticleID=2635, http://www.azom.com/Details.asp?ArticleID=2639.

Mason, R., Biomaterials – The Science and Biology Behind Biomaterials Research, *Materials World*, Vol. 5, No. 1, pp. 16-17, January 1997. See also: http://www.azom.com/details.asp?ArticleID=2102.

Mayes, A., Materials for Biomedical Applications (Lecture Notes), http://aka-ocw.mit.edu/OcwWeb/Materials-Science-and-Engineering/3-051JSpring2004/LectureNotes/index.htm, Cambridge, Massachusetts Institute of Technology, 2004.

Mikos, A.G., and Temenoff, J.S., Formation of highly porous biodegradable scaffolds for tissue engineering. *Electronic Journal of Biotechnology*, Vol. 3, No. 2, pp. 114-119, http://www.ejbiotechnology.info/content/vol3/issue2/full/5/5.pdf, 15 August 2000.

O'Brien, W.J., University of Michigan Biomaterials Properties Database. http://www.lib.umich.edu/dentlib/Dental_tables/intro.html. 45 tables of biomaterials properties drawn from 244 references. Primarily dental materials.

Picciolo, G.L., Hellman, K.B., and Johnson, P.C., Rationale and Justification for the Development of Standards. *Tissue Engineering*, Vol. 4, pp. (unknown), 1998. (also at http://www.fda.gov/cdrh/tisseng/te3.html).

RAND, Biomaterials Availability: Potential Effects on Medical Innovation and Health Care. *RAND Issue Paper IP-194*, January 2000. Available online at: http://www.rand.org/publications/IP/IP194/IP194.pdf

Ward, R., Segmented Polyurethanes for Medical Applications: History, Present, and Future, http://www.polymertech.com/pubs/abstract_1.html.

West, J.L., Biomaterials II: Education Within the BME Curriculum. http://summit.whitaker.org/white/biomat2.pdf, Arlington, VA: The Whitaker Foundation, December 2000.

Complete Bibliography – all sources considered for this study

Books

Anon., *Improving Medical Implant Performance Through Retrieval Information: Challenges and Opportunities*. National Institutes of Health, NIH Technology Assessment Conference Summary, January 10-12, 2000. Available online at: http://www.ncbi.nlm.nih.gov/books.

Anon., *Materials Science and Engineering for the 1990s: Maintaining Competitiveness in the Age of Materials*. 296 pp. Washington, DC: National Academy Press, 1989.

Anon., *Workshop on Standards for Biomedical Materials and Devices, NISTIR 6791*. 62 pp. Gaithersburg, MD: National Institute of Standards and Technology, 2001.

Black, J., and Hastings, G., eds., *Handbook of Biomaterial Properties*. 616 pp. Springer, 1998.

Black, J., *Biological Performance of Materials: Fundamentals of Biocompatibility*. 463 pp. Marcel Dekker, 1999.

Boretos, J.W., *Concise Guide to Biomedical Polymers*. 179 pp. Springfield IL: Charles C. Thomas, 1973.

Budinski, K.G., and Budinsky, M.K., *Engineering Materials: Properties and Selection*. Seventh edition. 818 pp. Prentice Hall, Upper Saddle River, NJ, 2002.

Davis, J.R., *Handbook of Materials for Medical Devices*. 341 pp. ASM International, 2004.

Dee, K.C., Puleo, D.A., and Bizios, R., *An Introduction to Tissue-Biomaterial Interactions*. 248 pp. Wiley-Liss, 2002.

Ducheyne, P., and Hastings, G.W., *Metallic and Ceramic Biomaterals: Volume I Structure*. Boca Raton, FL: CRC Press, Inc., 1984.

Gibson, L.J., and Ashby, M.F., *Cellular Solids: Structure and Properties*. Second edition. 510 pp. Cambridge: Cambridge University Press, 1997.

Lelah, Michael D., and Cooper, Stuart L., *Polyurethanes in Medicine*. 225 pp. CRC Press, Inc., Boca Raton, FL, 1986.

Munro, R.G., *Data Evaluation Theory and Practice for Materials Properties*. 128 pp. NIST Recommended Practice Guide Special Publication 960-11, Washington: U.S. Government Printing Office, 2003.

National Research Council, *Guide for the Care and Use of Laboratory Animals*. 140 pp. Washington, DC: National Academy Press, 1996.

Park, J.B., *Biomaterials*. Part IV of *The Biomedical Engineering Handbook*, Bronzino, J.D., Ed.-in-Chief, 194 pp., Boca Raton, FL: CRC Press, 1995.

Park, J.B., and Bronzino, J.D., eds., *Biomaterials: Principles and Applications*. 250 pp. Boca Raton, FL: CRC Press, 2003.

Park, J.B., and Lakes, R.S., *Biomaterials: an Introduction*. Second edition. 412 pp. Plenum Press, New York, NY, 1992.

Ratner, B.D., Hoffman, A.S., Schoen, F.J., and Lemons, J.E., *Biomaterials Science: an Introduction to Materials in Medicine*. 484 pp. Academic Press, San Diego, CA, 1996.

Ratner, B.D., Hoffman, A.S., Schoen, F.J., and Lemons, J.E., *Biomaterials Science: an Introduction to Materials in Medicine, 2nd Edition*. 851 pp. Academic Press, San Diego, CA, 2004.

Silver, F.H., *Biomaterials, Medical Devices and Tissue Engineering: an Integrated Approach*. 303 pp. London: Chapman & Hall, 1994.

Von Recum, A.F., ed., *Handbook of Biomaterials Evaluation: Scientific, Technical, and Clinical Testing of Implant Materials*. 700 pp. Philadelphia, PA: Taylor & Francis, 1999.

Williams, D.F., ed., *Definitions in Biomaterials. Proceedings of a Consensus Conference of the European Society for Biomaterials, Chester, England, March 3-5, 1986*. 72 pp. Amsterdam: Elsevier Science Publishers B.V., 1987.

Williams, D.F., ed., Medical and Dental Materials, Vol. 14 of *Materials Science and Technology: a Comprehensive Treatment*. 441 pp. New York: VCH Publishers, Inc., 1992.

Articles

Biomaterials – Data and Other Needs

Addadi, L., and Safinya, C.R., Biomaterials: editorial overview. *Current Opinion in Solid State & Materials Science*, Vol. 2, pp. 325-329, 1997.

Aksay, A., and Weiner, S., Biomaterials: Is this really a field of research? *Current Opinion in Solid State & Materials Science*, Vol. 3, pp. 219-220, 1998.

Andrade, J.D., Needs, Problems, and Opportunities in Biomaterials and Biocompatibility. *Clinical Materials*, Vol. 11, pp. 19-23, 1992.

Anon., *Medical Implant Information, Performance, and Policies Workshop Final Report*, Rockville, MD, September 19-20, 2002, 27 pp., http://www.nbib1.nih.gov/events/BMIS/BMIS2002.htm.

Barenberg, S.A., Abridged report of the committee to survey the needs and opportunities for the biomaterials industry. *Journal of Biomedical Materials Research*, Vol. 22, pp. 1267-1291, 1988.

Barenberg, S.A., Report of the Committee to Survey Needs and Opportunities for the Biomaterials Industry. *MRS Bulletin*, Vol. 16, pp. 26-32, September 1991.

Brunsky, J.B., Biomaterials and Medical Implant Science. *International Journal of Oral & Maxillofacial Implants*, Vol. 10, No. 6, pp. 649-650, 1995.

Eisenberger, P., Rekow, D., Jelinski, L.W., Marlow, D.E., McKinlay, S.M., Meyer, A.E., Potvin, A.R., Ratner, B.D., Watson, J.T., Braveman, N., Cassatt, J., Didisheim, P., Holloway, C., and Panagis, J.S., Biomaterials and medical implant science: Present and future perspectives: A summary report. *Journal of Biomedical Materials Research*, Vol. 32, pp. 143-147, 1996.

Mueller, E.P., and Barenberg, S.A., Biomaterials in an Emerging National Materials Science Agenda. *MRS Bulletin*, Vol. 16, pp. 86-87, September 1991.

Ratner, B.D., New ideas in biomaterials science – a path to engineered biomaterials. *Journal of Biomedical Materials Research*, Vol. 27, pp. 837-850, 1993.

Safinya, C.R., and Addadi, L., Biomaterials: editorial overview. *Current Opinion in Solid State & Materials Science*, Vol. 1, pp. 387-391, 1996.

Spector, M., Biomaterials: Taming the beast. *Journal of Biomedical Materials Research*, Vol. 26, pp. 1-5, 1992.

Tesk, J.A., NIST workshop on needs for reference biomaterials. *Journal of Biomedical Materials Research*, Vol. 51, pp. 155-156, 2000.

Tesk, J.A., NIST Workshop on Reference Data for the Properties of Biomaterials. *Journal of Biomedical Materials Research (Applied Biomaterials)*, Vol. 58, pp. 463-466, 2001.

Tesk, J.A., Reference Data and Materials Needed. *Government News*, Vol. 22, No. 6, p. 11, 2001.

Tesk, J.A., Reference Materials, Reference Data Committee. *Biomaterials Forum*, Vol. 24, No. 2, p. ?, 1 September 2002.

Watson, J.T., NIH Biomaterials and Medical Implant Science Coordinating Committee. *Journal of Biomedical Materials Research*, Vol. 36, p. 283, 1997.

Biomaterials – General

Agrawal, C.M., Reconstructing the Human Body Using Biomaterials. *JOM*, Vol. 50, No. 1, pp. 31-35, January 1998.

Anderson, K.J., From Willow Wood to Silicone Rubber. *MRS Bulletin*, Vol. 16, p. 90, September 1991.

Anon., Biomaterials – Densities of Biomaterials and Some Other Related Materials. http://www.azom.com/details.asp?ArticleID=1413, 2004.

Anon., Biomedical Materials. *Chemistry for Health*, (briefing paper #2), 4 pp., http://www.rsc.org/pdf/publicaf/chbp2.pdf, London, Royal Society of Chemistry, March 1999.

Anon., Materials Selection for Total Hip Replacement. http://www.materials.qmul.ac.uk/casestud/implants, London, Department of Materials, Queen Mary, University of London, 2004.

Anon., Medical Materials. *Advanced Materials & Processes*, Vol. 160, No. 9, pp. 24-27, September 2002.

Anon., Orthopaedic Biomaterials Market Review. http://www.azom.com/details.asp?ArticleID=1361, 2004.

Anon., Survey of Biomedical Materials. *Advanced Materials & Processes*, Vol. 159, No. 9, pp. 26-29, September 2001.

Ashammakhi, N., From Past to Present and Future is Today: From Inert to Multifunctional Biomaterials. *Journal of Craniofacial Surgery*, Vol. 15, No. 6, p. 897, November 2004.

Ashammakhi, N., Reactions to Biomaterials: the Good, the Bad, and Ideas for Developing New Therapeutic Approaches. *Journal of Craniofacial Surgery*, Vol. 16, No. 2, pp. 195-196, March 2005.

Ball, P., Made to measure: new materials for the 21st century, Chapter 5: Biomedical Materials, pp. 209-243, Princeton, NJ: Princeton University Press, 1997.

Berman, H. M., Olson, W. K., Beveridge, D. L., Westbrook, J., Gelbin, A., Demeny, T., Hsieh, S.-H., Srinivasan, A. R., and Schneider, B.: The Nucleic Acid Database: A Comprehensive Relational Database of

Three-Dimensional Structures of Nucleic Acids. *Biophysical Journal*, Vol. 63, pp. 751-759, 1992. Maintained online at: http://ndbserver.rutgers.edu/.

Berman, H.M, Westbrook, J., Feng, Z., Gilliland, G., Bhat, T.N., Weissig, H., Shindyalov, I.N., and Bourne, P.E.: The Protein Data Bank. *Nucleic Acids Research*, 28 pp. 235-242, 2000. Maintained online at: http://www.rcsb.org/pdb/.

Black, M.M., Cardiovascular applications of biomaterials and implants – an overview. *Journal of Medical Engineering & Technology*, Vol. 19, No. 5, pp. 151-157, September/October 1995.

Black, M.M., van Noort, R., and Drury, P.J., Medical Applications of Biomaterials. *Physics in Technology*, Vol. 13, pp. 50-56,65, 1982.

Bonfield, W., and Tanner, K.E., Biomaterials – a new generation. *Materials World*, Vol. 5, No. 1., pp. 18-20, January 1997.

Bruck, S.D., Current and Future Directions of Biomedical Materials Research. *Journal of Long-Term Effects of Medical Implants*, Vol. 7, No. 2, pp. 115-117, 1997.

Bruck, S.D., Materials or biomaterials? *The International Journal of Artificial Organs*, Vol. 13, No. 8, pp. 469-471, 1990.

Burg, T., and Standard, O., *Materials for Biomedical Engineering*, Student Notes, School of Materials Science and Engineering, University of New South Wales, 15 pp., http://www.materials.unsw.edu.au/news/biomed-s.pdf, 2001.

Burg, T., and Standard, O., *Materials for Biomedical Engineering*, Teacher Reference, School of Materials Science and Engineering, University of New South Wales, 22 pp., http://www.materials.unsw.edu.au/news/biomed-t.pdf, 2001.

Bush, R.B., A Bibliography of Monographic Works on Biomaterials and Biocompatibility. *Journal of Applied Biomaterials*, Vol. 4, pp. 195-209, 1993.

Bush, R.B., A Bibliography of Monographic Works on Biomaterials and Biocompatibility: Update. *Journal of Biomedical Materials Research (Applied Biomaterials)*, Vol. 33, pp. 107-113, 1996.

Bush, R.B., A Bibliography of Monographic Works on Biomaterials and Biocompatibility: Update II. *Journal of Biomedical Materials Research (Applied Biomaterials)*, Vol. 48, pp. 335-341, 1999.

Donachie, M., Biomaterials. In: *ASM Metals Handbook, Desk Edition, 2nd ed.*, pp. 702-709, Materials Park, OH: ASM International, 1998.

Eisenbarth, E., and Morlock, M., Biomaterials. 19 pp., http://www.tu.harburg.de/bim/lecture/biomaterials/biomaterials.2004.02.pdf.

Gibbons, D.F., Biomedical Materials. *Annual Review of Biomedical Engineering*, pp. 367-375, 1975.

Gilliland, G.L., Tung, M., Blakeslee, D.M. and Ladner, J. 1994. The Biological Macromolecule Crystallization Database, Version 3.0: New Features, Data, and the NASA Archive for Protein Crystal Growth Data. *Acta Crystallogr.* D50 408-413. Maintained online at http://wwwbmcd.nist.gov:8080/bmcd/bmcd.html.

Granja, P.L., The Biomaterials Network (Biomat.net): Objectives, Activities and Future Goals. 8 pp. Available online at http://www.biocities2001.de/biocities_granja.pdf.

Hanker, J.S., and Giammara, B.L., Biomaterials and Biomedical Devices. *Science*, Vol. 242, pp. 885-892, 11 November 1988.

Helmus, M.N., Overview of Biomedical Materials. *MRS Bulletin*, Vol. 16, pp. 33-38, September 1991.

Hench, L.L., Biomaterials: a forecast for the future. *Biomaterials*, Vol. 19, pp. 1419-1423, 1998.

Hench, L.L., and Polak, J.M., Third-Generation Biomedical Materials. *Science*, Vol. 295, pp. 1014, 1016-1017, 8 February 2002.

Hotter, D.S., Band-Aids for Broken Bones. *Machine Design*, pp. 39-44, 4 April 1996.

Jones, J.R., and Hench, L.L., Biomedical materials for new millennium: perspective on the future. *Materials Science and Technology*, Vol. 17, pp. 891-900, August 2001.

Katz, J.L., Biomaterials in the 21st Century? *Journal of Rehabilitation Research and Development*, Vol. 32, No. 3, pp. vii-viii, 1995.

Katz, J.L., Biomaterials in the 21st Century Revisited! *Journal of Rehabilitation Research and Development*, Vol. 35, No. 2, pp. ix-xi, 1998.

Kohn, J., New approaches to biomaterials design. *Nature Materials*, Vol. 3, pp. 745-747, November 2004.

Lakes, R., Materials with structural hierarchy. *Nature*, Vol. 361, pp. 511-515, 11 February 1993.

Langer, R., Biomaterials: Status, Challenges, and Perspectives. *AIChE Journal*, Vol. 46, No. 7, pp. 1286-1289, July 2000.

Langer, R., and Tirrell, D.A., Designing materials for biology and medicine. *Nature*, Vol. 428, pp. 487-492, 1 April 2004.

Lemons, J.E., Biomaterials, Biomechanics, Tissue Healing, and Immediate-Function Dental Implants. *Journal of Oral Implantology*, Vol. 30, No. 5, pp. 318-324, 2004.

Lemons, J.E., Dental implant biomaterials. *Journal of the American Dental Association*, Vol. 121, No. 6, pp. 716-719, December 1990.

Lyman, D.J., and Seare, Jr., W.J., Biomedical Materials in Surgery. *Annual Review of Biomedical Engineering*, pp. 415-433, 1974.

Mason, R., Biomaterials – The Science and Biology Behind Biomaterials Research, *Materials World*, Vol. 5, No. 1, pp. 16-17, January 1997. See also: http://www.azom.com/details.asp?ArticleID=2102.

Mayes, A., Materials for Biomedical Applications (Lecture Notes), 277 pp., http://aka-ocw.mit.edu/OcwWeb/Materials-Science-and-Engineering/3-051JSpring2004/LectureNotes/index.htm, Cambridge, Massachusetts Institute of Technology, 2004.

Meaney, D.F., Mechanical Properties of Implantable Biomaterials. *Clinics in Podiatric Medicine and Surgery*, Vol. 12, No. 3, pp. 363-384, July 1995.

Mraz, S.J., The human body shop. *Machine Design*, pp. 90-94, 7 November 1991.

Nomura, T., Shingaki, S., and Nakajima, T., Current Evaluation of Dental Implants: A Review of the Literature. *Journal of Long-Term Effects of Medical Implants*, Vol. 8, No. 3-4, pp. 175-192, 1998.

Ouellette, J., Biomaterials Facilitate Medical Breakthroughs. *The Industrial Physicist*, Vol. 7, No. 5, pp. 18-21, October/November 2001.

Peppas, N.A., and Langer, R., New Challenges in Biomaterials. *Science*, Vol. 263, pp. 1715-1720, 25 March 1994.

Perel, M.L., Questions That Have Yet to be Answered. *Dental Implantology Update*, Vol. 3, No. 11, p. 88, November 1992.

Pilliar, R.M., Davies, J.E., and Smith, D.C., The Bone-Biomaterial Interface for Load-Bearing Implants. *MRS Bulletin*, Vol. 16, pp. 55-61, September 1991.

Ratner, B.D., Replacing and Renewing: Synthetic Materials, Biomimetics, and Tissue Engineering in Implant Dentistry. *Journal of Dental Education*, Vol. 65, No. 12, pp. 1340-1347, December 2001.

Ratner, B.D., and Bryant, S.J., Biomaterials: Where We Have Been and Where We Are Going. *Annual Review of Biomedical Engineering*, Vol. 6, pp. 41-75, 2004.

Smith, G.K., Orthopaedic Biomaterials. In: *Textbook of Small Animal Orthopaedics*, Newton, C.D., and Nunamaker, D.M., eds., Ithaca, NY: International Veterinary Information Service, 5 pp., 1985. See also: http://cal.vet.upenn.edu/saortho/chapter_13/13mast.htm.

Spector, M., and Yannis, I.V., Chapter 8: Design Parameters. 12 pp., http://ocw.mit.edu/NR/rdonlyres/Mechanical-Engineering/2-782JDesign-of-Medical-Devices-and-ImplantsSpring2003/3DEBC7B6-8C33-4167-8C86-FAE569B275C9/0/chapter_8.pdf, Cambridge: Massachusetts Institute of Technology, 2003.

Suh, H., Recent Advances in Biomaterials. *Yonsei Medical Journal*, Vol. 39, No. 2, pp. 87-96, 1998.

Tanner, K.E., Modulus Matched Materials for Medical Applications. *Materials Science Forum*, Vols. 440-441, pp. 19-28, 2003.

Teoh. S.H., Fatigue of biomaterials: a review. *International Journal of Fatigue*, Vol. 22, pp. 825-837, 2000.

Biomaterials – Other Topics, e.g., Availability, Biocompatibility, Education, Nanotechnology, Standardization, Surface Science, Tissue Engineering

Alivisatos, A.P., Barbara, P.F., Castleman, A.W., Chang, J., Dixon, D.A., Klein, M.L., McLendon, G.L., Miller, J.S., Ratner, M.A., Rossky, P.J., Stupp, S.I., and Thompson, M.E., From Molecules to Materials: Current Trends and Future Directions. *Advanced Materials*, Vol. 10, No. 16, pp. 1297-1336, 1998.

Anderson, J.M., Biological responses to materials. *Annual Review of Materials Research*, Vol. 31, pp. 81-110, 2001.

Andrade, J., Biomaterials I: Past, Present and Future. http://summit.whitaker.org/white/biomat1.pdf, Arlington, VA: The Whitaker Foundation, December 2000.

Black, J., "Safe" biomaterals. *Journal of Biomedical Materials Research*, Vol. 29, pp. 791-792, 1995.

Borgersen, S., Safety and Innovation in Biomedical Device Design: the Increasing Role of Simulation. *The Journal of Virtual Product Development*, Vol. 2, Spring 2004, http://www.coe.org/newsnet/sept04/.

Bruck, S.D., and Mueller, E.P., Reference standards for implantable materials: problems and needs. *Medical Progress through Technology*, Vol. 15, pp. 5-20, 1989.

Castner, D.G., and Ratner, B.D., Biomedical surface science: Foundations to frontiers. *Surface Science*, Vol. 500, pp. 28-60, 2002.

Chapekar, M.S., Tissue Engineering: Challenges and Opportunities. *Journal of Biomedical Materials Research (Applied Biomaterials)*, Vol. 53, pp. 617-620, 2000.

Cohen, S., and Leor, J., Rebuilding Broken Hearts. *Scientific American*, Vol. 291, No. 5, November 2004.

Daniels, A.U., Applied Biomaterials Standards Report. *Journal of Biomedical Materials Research: Applied Biomaterials*, Vol. 23, No. A1, pp. 9-11, 1989.

Daniels, A.U., Applied Biomaterials Standards Report. *Journal of Biomedical Materials Research: Applied Biomaterials*, Vol. 21, No. A3, pp. 247-250, 1987.

de Mol, B.A.J.M., and van Gaalen, G.L., The Editor's Corner: Biomaterials Crisis in the Medical Device Industry: Is Litigation the Only Cause? *Journal of Biomedical Materials Research (Applied Biomaterials)*, Vol. 33, pp. 53-54, 1996.

Galletti, P.M., Biomaterials availability in the U.S. *Journal of Biomedical Materials Research*, Vol. 32, pp. 289-291, 1996.

Galletti, P.M., Brash, J.L., Keller, K.H., La Farge, G., Mason, R.G., Pierce, W.S., and Reynolds, J.A., Report of the Task Force on Biomaterials to the Cardiology Advisory Committee of the NHLBI. *Cardiovascular Diseases, Bulletin of the Texas Heart Institute*, Vol. 5, No. 3, pp. 293-314, September 1978.

Galletti, P.M., Hellman, K.B., and Nerem, R.M., Tissue Engineering: From Basic Science to Products. *Tissue Engineering*, Vol. 1, No. 2, pp. 147-161, 1995.

Griffith, L.G., and Naughton, G., Tissue Engineering – Current Challenges and Expanding Opportunities. *Science*, Vol. 295, pp. 1009-1014, 8 February 2002.

Helmus, M.N., Overview and Introduction: Unique Aspects of Biomaterials in the Safety and Efficacy of Medical Implant Devices. Chapter 1 in *Biomaterials in the Design and Reliability of Medical Devices*, pp. 1-52, Kluwer Academic / Plenum, 2003.

Hench, L.L., Bioactive materials: The potential for tissue regeneration. *Journal of Biomedical Materials Research*, Vol. 41, No. 4, pp. 511-518, 1998.

Hench, L.L., Bioceramics and the origin of life. *Journal of Biomedical Materials Research*, Vol. 23, pp. 685-703, 1989.

Homsy, C.A., Bio-Compatibility in Selection of Materials for Implantation. *Journal of Biomedical Materials Research*, Vol. 4, pp. 341-356, 1970.

Hubbell, J.A., Biomaterials in Tissue Engineering. *Biotechnology*, Vol. 13, pp. 565-576, June 1995.

Hulbert, S.F., The teaching of biomaterials. *Journal of Biomedical Materials Research*, Vol. 57, pp. 475-476, 2001.

Karp, J.M., Friis, E.A., Dee, K.C., and Winet, H., Opinions and trends in biomaterials education: Report of a 2003 Society for Biomaterials survey. *Journal of Biomedical Materials Research*, Vol. 70A, pp. 1-9, 2004.

Lambert, R.D., and Anthony, M.E., Standardization in Orthopaedics: The Growth and Activities of ASTM's Athroplasty Subcommittee. *ASTM Standardization News*, Vol. 23, No. 8, pp. 22-29, August 1995.

Langer, R., and Vacanti, J.P., Tissue Engineering: The Challenges Ahead. *Scientific American*, Vol. 280, pp. 86-89, April 1999.

Langer, R., and Vacanti, J.P., Tissue Engineering. *Science*, Vol. 260, pp. 920-926, 14 May 1993.

Lavik, E., and Langer, R., Tissue engineering: current state and perspectives. *Applied Microbiology and Biotechnology*, Vol. 65, pp. 1-8, 2004.

Letić-Gavrilović, A., Scandurra, R., and Abe, K., Genetic Potential of Interfacial Guided Osteogenesis in Implant Devices. *Dental Materials Journal*, Vol. 19, No. 2, pp. 99-132, 2000.

Ottensmeyer, M.P., TeMPeST I-D: An Instrument for Measuring Solid Organ Soft Tissue Properties. *Experimental Techniques*, Vol. 26, pp. 48-50, May/June 2002.

Pankhurst, Q.A., Connolly, J., Jones, S.K., and Dobson, J., Applications of magnetic nanoparticles in biomedicine. *Journal of Physics D: Applied Physics*, Vol. 36, pp. R167-R181, 2003.

Picciolo, G.L., Hellman, K.B., and Johnson, P.C., Meeting report: Tissue engineered medical products standards: The time is ripe. *Tissue Engineering*, Vol. 4, pp. 5-7, Spring 1998. (also published online as: Rationale and Justification for the Development of Standards, at http://www.fda.gov/cdrh/tisseng/te3.html).

Puleo, D.A., and Nanci, A., Understanding and controlling the bone-implant interface. *Biomaterials*, Vol. 20, pp. 2311-2321, 1999.

RAND, Biomaterials Availability: Potential Effects on Medical Innovation and Health Care. *RAND Issue Paper IP-194*, January 2000. 61 pp. Available online at: http://www.rand.org/publications/IP/IP194/IP194.pdf.

Ratner, B.D., Surface modification of polymers: chemical, biological and surface analytical challenges. *Biosensors & Bioelectronics*, Vol. 10, pp. 797-804, 1995.

Remes, A., and Williams, D.F., Review: Immune response in biocompatibility. *Biomaterials*, Vol. 13, No. 11, pp. 731-743.

Salata, O.V., Applications of nanoparticles in biology and medicine. *Journal of Nanobiotechnology*, Vol. 2, No. 3, pp. 1-6, 2004.

Salgado, A.J., Coutinho, O.P., and Reis, R.L., Bone Tissue Engineering: State of the Art and Future Trends. *Macromolecular Bioscience*, Vol. 4, pp. 743-765, 2004.

St. John, K.R., Biocompatibility Testing for Medical Implant Materials. *ASTM Standardization News*, Vol. 22, No. 3, pp. 46-49, March 1994.

Shin, H., Jo, S., and Mikos, A.G., Biomimetic materials for tissue engineering. *Biomaterials*, Vol. 24, pp. 4353-4364, 2003.

Tyas. M.J., Dental materials science – the maintenance of standards. *Journal of Oral Rehabilitation*, Vol. 18, No. 1, pp. 105-110, 1991.

Vander Sloten, J., Labey, L., Van Audekercke, R., and Van der Perre, G., Materials selection and design for orthopaedic implants with improved long-term performance. *Biomaterials*, Vol. 19, pp. 1455-1459, 1998.

Wallin, R.F., Improving Biocompatibility Standards for the Global Market. *Medical Device & Diagnostic Industry*, pp. 36-42, December 1996.

West, J.L., Biomaterials II: Education Within the BME Curriculum. 3 pp. Available at: http://summit.whitaker.org/white/biomat2.pdf, Arlington, VA: The Whitaker Foundation, December 2000.

Williams, D.F., Review: Tissue-biomaterial interactions. *Journal of Materials Science*, Vol. 22, pp. 3421-3445, 1987.

Ceramics

Anon., Calcium Phosphate Biomaterials – Solubility of Calcium Phosphates. http://www.azom.com/details.asp?ArticleID=2140, 2004.

Anon., Cementing new applications in bone repair. *Materials World*, Vol. 12, No. 3, p. 12, March 2004.

Anon., Sodium Citrate Modified Calcium Phosphate Cement for Bone Repair Applications. *Materials World*, Vol. 12, No. 3, p. 12, March 2004. See also: http://www.azom.com/details.asp?ArticleID=2528.

Binner, J., and Sambrook, R.; Break out the bubbly – new ceramic foams. *Materials World*, Vol. 10, No. 2, pp. 13-15, February 2002. See also: http://www.azom.com/details.asp?ArticleID=1869.

Burger, W., Richter, H.G., Piconi, C., Vatteroni, R., Cittadini, A., and Boccalari, M., New Y-TZP powders for medical grade zirconia. *Journal of Materials Science: Materials in Medicine*, Vol. 8, pp. 113-118, 1997.

Catledge, S.A., Fries, M.D., Vohra, Y.K., Lacefield, W.R., Lemons, J.E., Woodard, S., and Venugopalan, R., Nanostructured Ceramics for Biomedical Implants. *Journal of Nanoscience and Nanotechnology*, Vol. 2, No. 3/4, pp. 293-312, 2002.

Christel, P., Meunier, A., and Heller, M., Mechanical properties and short-term *in-vivo* evaluation of yttrium-oxide-partially-stabilized zirconia. *Journal of Biomedical Materials Research*, Vol. 23, pp. 45-61, 1989.

Cordingley, R., Kohan, L., Ben-Nissan, B., and Pezzotti, G., Alumina and Zirconia Bioceramics in Orthopaedic Applications. *Journal of the Australasian Ceramic Society*, Vol. 39, No. 1, pp. 20-28, 2003. See also: http://www.azom.com/Details.asp?ArticleID=2160, http://www.azom.com/Details.asp?ArticleID=2161.

De Diego, M.A., Coleman, N.J., and Hench, L.L., Tensile Properties of Bioactive Fibers for Tissue Engineering Applications. *Journal of Biomedical Materials Research (Applied Biomaterials)*, Vol. 53, pp. 199-203, 2000.

Doremus, R.H., Review: Bioceramics. *Journal of Materials Science*, Vol. 27, pp. 285-297, 1992.

Dubok, V.A., Bioceramics – Yesterday, Today, Tomorrow. *Powder Metallurgy and Metal Ceramics*, Vol. 39, Nos. 7-8, pp. 381-394, 2000.

Grenoble, D.E., Katz, J.L, Dunn, K.L., Gilmore, R.S., and Murty, K.L., The Elastic Properties of Hard Tissues and Apatites. *Journal of Biomedical Materials Research*, Vol. 6, pp. 221-233, 1972.

Gross, K., Bioceramics – An Overview Including Calcium Phosphates, Hydroxyapatite, Alumina, Zirconia, and Pyrolytic Carbon. http://www.azom.com/details.asp?ArticleID=1743, 2004.

Hench, L.L., Bioactive Glasses and Glass-Ceramics. *Materials Science Forum*, Vol. 293, pp. 37-64, 1999.

Hench, L.L., Bioactive materials: The potential for tissue regeneration. *Journal of Biomedical Materials Research*, Vol. 41, No. 4, pp. 511-518, 1998.

Hench, L.L., Bioceramics. *Journal of the American Ceramic Society*, Vol. 81, No. 7, pp. 1705-1728, 1998.

Hench, L.L., Bioceramics: From Concept to Clinic. *Journal of the American Ceramic Society*, Vol. 74, No. 7, pp. 1487-1510, 1991.

Hench, L.L., Medical Materials for the Next Millenium. *MRS Bulletin*, Vol. 24, No. 5, pp. 13-19, May 1999.

Hench, L.L., Medical and Scientific Products, in *Ceramics and Glasses, Vol. 4, Engineered Materials Handbook*. ASM International, pp. 1007-1013, 1991.

Hench, L.L., and Wilson, J., Bioceramics. *MRS Bulletin*, Vol. 16, pp. 62-74, September 1991.

Heness, G., and Ben-Nissan, B., Innovative Bioceramics. *Materials Forum*, Vol. 27, pp. 104-114, 2004. See also: http://www.azom.com/Details.asp?ArticleID=2632, http://www.azom.com/Details.asp?ArticleID=2630, http://www.azom.com/Details.asp?ArticleID=2635, http://www.azom.com/Details.asp?ArticleID=2639.

Kaae, J.L., Structure and Mechanical Properties of Isotropic Pyrolytic Carbons Deposited Below 1600 °C. *Journal of Nuclear Materials*, Vol. 38, pp. 42-50, 1971.

Kelly, J.R., Ceramics in Restorative and Prosthetic Dentistry. *Annual Review of Materials Science*, Vol. 27, pp. 443-468, 1997.

Ni, M., and Ratner, B.D., Nacre surface transformation to hydroxyapatite in a phosphate buffer solution. *Biomaterials*, Vol. 24, pp. 4323-4331.

Rawlings, R.D., Bioactive Glasses and Glass-Ceramics. *Clinical Materials*, Vol. 14, pp. 155-179, 1993.

Ritchie, R.O., Fatigue and Fracture of Pyrolytic Carbon: A Damage-Tolerant Approach to Structural Integrity and Life Prediction in "Ceramic" Heart Valve Prostheses. *Journal of Heart Valve Disease*, Vol. 5, Suppl. I, pp. S9-S31, 1996.

Sepulveda, P., Ortega, F.S., Innocentini, M.D.M., and Pandofelli, V.C., Properties of Highly Porous Hydroxyapatite Obtained by the Gelcasting of Foams. *Journal of the American Ceramic Society*, Vol. 83, No. 12, pp. 3021-3024, 2000.

Shackelford, J.F., Bioceramics – An Historical Perspective. *Materials Science Forum*, Vol. 293, pp. 1-4, 1999.

Shackelford, J.F., Bioceramics – Current Status and Future Trends. *Materials Science Forum*, Vol. 293, pp. 99-106, 1999.

Suchanek, W., and Yoshimura, M., Processing and properties of hydroxyapatite-based biomaterials for use as hard tissue replacement implants. *Journal of Materials Research*, Vol. 13, No. 1, pp. 94-117, January 1998.

Thamaraiselvi, T.V., and Rajeswari, S., Biological Evaluation of Bioceramic Materials – A Review. *Trends in Biomaterials & Artifical Organs*, Vol. 18, No. 1, pp. 9-17, 2004.

Zhang, Y., and Lawn, B., Long-Term Strength of Ceramics for Biomedical Applications. *Journal of Biomedical Materials Research Part B: Applied Biomaterials*, Vol. 69B, No. 2, pp. 166-172, 2004.

Metals

Anon., Cobalt-Chrome Stents Receive FDA Approval, http://www.azom.com/details.asp?ArticleID=2144, 2004.

Anon., Data Sheet No. 14: Titanium for Medical Applications, Titanium Information Group, http://www.titaniuminfogroup.co.uk/i/pdfs/data14.pdf, 2001.

Anon., Gold – Applications and Developments in the Electronics, Biomaterials and Catalysis. *Materials World*, Vol. 11, No. 2, pp. 12-14, February 2003. See also http://www.azom.com/details.asp?ArticleID=1899, 2004.

Anon., Titanium Alloys – Ti6Al7Nb Properties and Applications, http://www.azom.com/details.asp?ArticleID=2064, 2004.

Anon., Titanium and Titanium Alloys as Biomaterials, http://www.azom.com/Details.asp?ArticleID=1520, 2004.

Cruickshanks-Boyd, D.W., and Lock, W.R., Fracture toughness of dental amalgams. *Biomaterials*, Vol. 4, pp. 234-242, 1983.

Davidson, J.A., Mishra, A.K., Kovacs, P., and Poggie, R.A., New Surface-Hardened, Low-Modulus, Corrosion-Resistant Ti-13Nb-13Zr Alloy for Total Hip Arthroplasty. *Bio-Medical Materials and Engineering*, Vol. 4, No. 3, pp. 231-243, 1994.

Devine, T.M., and Wulff, J., Cast vs. Wrought Cobalt-Chromium Surgical Implant Alloys. *Journal of Biomedical Materials Research*, Vol. 9, pp. 151-167, 1975.

Fraker, A.C., and Ruff, A.W., Metallic surgical implants: state of the art. *Journal of Metals*, Vol. 29, pp. 22-28, May 1977.

Frary, M., Abkowitz, S., Abkowitz, S.M., and Dunand, D.C., Microstructure and mechanical properties of Ti/W and Ti-6Al-4V/W composites fabricated by powder-metallurgy. *Materials Science and Engineering*, Vol. A344, pp. 103-112, 2003.

Gil, F.J., and Planell, J.A., Shape memory alloys for medical applications. *Proceedings of the Institute of Mechanical Engineers, Journal of engineering in medicine*, Vol. 212, Part H, pp. 473-488, 1998.

Hamman, G., and Bardos, D.I., Metallographic Quality Control or Orthopaedic Implants, in *Metallography as a Quality Control Tool*, McCall, J.L., and French, P.M., eds., pp. 221-245, Plenum Press, New York, 1980.

He, G., Eckert, J., Dai, Q.L., Sui, M.L., Löser, W., Hagiwara, M., and Ma, E., Nanostructured Ti-based multi-component alloys with potential for biomedical applications. *Biomaterials*, Vol. 24, pp. 5115-5120, 2003.

Hille, G.H., Titanium for Surgical Implants. *Journal of Materials*, Vol. 1, No. 2, pp. 373-383, June 1966.

Ito, A., Okazaki, Y., Tateishi, T., and Ito, Y., *In vitro* biocompatibility, mechanical properties, and corrosion resistance of Ti-Zr-Nb-Ta-Pd and Ti-Sn-Nb-Ta-Pd alloys. *Journal of Biomedical Materials Research*, Vol. 29, pp. 893-900, 1995.

Kobayashi, E., Doi, H., Yoneyama, T., Hamanaka, H., Gibson, I.R., Best, S.M., Shelton, J.C., and Bonfield, W., Influence of aging heat treatment on mechanical properties of biomedical Ti-Zr based ternary alloys containing niobium. *Journal of Materials Science: Materials in Medicine*, Vol. 9, pp. 625-630, 1998.

Kobayashi, E., Matsumoto, S., Doi, H., Yoneyama, T., and Hamanaka, H., Mechanical properties of the binary titanium-zirconium alloys and their potential for biomedical materials. *Journal of Biomedical Materials Research*, Vol. 29, pp. 943-950, 1995.

Kuroda, D., Niinomi, M., Morinaga, M., Kato, Y., and Yashiro, T., Design and mechanical properties of new β type titanium alloys for implant materials. *Materials Science and Engineering*, Vol. A243, pp. 244-249, 1998.

Kusy, R.P., and Greenberg, A.R., Dynamic mechanical properties of amalgams. *Journal of Biomedical Materials Research*, Vol. 15, pp. 47-59, 1981.

Lemons, J.E., and Lucas, L.C., Properties of Biomaterials. *Journal of Athroplasty*, Vol. 1, No. 2, pp. 143-147, June 1986.

Long, M., and Rack, H.J., Titanium alloys in total joint replacement – a materials science perspective. *Biomaterials*, Vol. 19, pp. 1621-1639, 1998.

Niinomi, M., Recent Metallic Materials for Biomedical Applications. *Metallurgical and Materials Transactions A*, Vol. 33A, pp. 477-486, March 2002.

Niinomi, M., Mechanical properties of biomedical titanium alloys. *Materials Science and Engineering*, Vol. A243, pp. 231-236, 1998.

Niinomi, M., Kuroda, D., Fukunaga, K., Morinaga, M., Kato, Y., Yashiro, T., and Suzuki, A., Corrosion wear fracture of new β type biomedical titanium alloys. *Materials Science and Engineering*, Vol. A263, pp. 193-199, 1999.

Pankhurst, Q.A., Connolly, J., Jones, S.K., and Dobson, J., Applications of magnetic nanoparticles in biomedicine. *Journal of Physics D: Applied Physics*, Vol. 36, pp. R167-R181, 2003.

Pilliar, R.M., Modern metal processing for improved load-bearing surgical implants. *Biomaterials*, Vol. 12, pp. 95-100, 1991.

Pilliar, R.M., and Weatherly, G.C., Developments in Implant Alloys. *CRC Critical Reviews in Biocompatibility*, Vol. 1, No. 4, pp. 371-403, 1985.

Rodriguez, D., Manero, J.M., Gil, F.J., and Planell, J.A., Low cycle fatigue behavior of Ti6Al4V thermochemically nitrided for its use in hip prostheses. *Journal of Materials Science: Materials in Medicine*, Vol. 12, pp. 935-937, 2001.

Sato, H., Kikuchi, M., Komatsu, M., Okuno, O., and Okabe, T., Mechanical properties of cast Ti-Hf alloys. *Journal of Biomedical Materials Research Part B: Applied Biomaterials*, Vol. 72B, No. 2, pp. 362-367, 2005.

Thomann, U.I., and Uggowitzer, P.J., Wear corrosion behavior of biocompatible austenitic stainless steels. *Wear*, Vol. 230, pp. 48-58.

Waterstrat, R.M., Brushing Up on the History of Intermetallics in Dentistry. *JOM*, Vol. 42, pp. 8-14, March 1990.

Wen, C.E., Yamada, Y., Shimojima, K., Chino, Y., Asahina, T., and Mabuchi, M., Processing and mechanical properties of autogenous titanium implant materials. *Journal of Materials Science: Materials in Medicine*, Vol. 13, pp. 397-401, 2002.

Polymers

Anderson, D.G., Burdick, J.A., and Langer, R., Smart Biomaterials. *Science*, Vol. 305, pp. 1923-1924, 24 September 2004.

Anon., Supplier Data – Polyhydroxybutyrate – (PHB) Biopolymer (Goodfellow), http://www.azom.com/details.asp?ArticleID=1881, 2004.

Boretos, J.W., and Pierce, W.S., Segmented Polyurethane: A New Elastomer for Biomedical Applications. *Science*, Vol. 158, pp. 1481-1482, 15 December 1967.

Boretos, J.W., and Pierce, W.S., Segmented Polyurethane: A Polyether Polymer – An Initial Evaluation for Biomedical Applications. *Journal of Biomedical Materials Research*, Vol. 2, pp. 121-130, 1968.

Braley, S., The Chemistry and Properties of the Medical-Grade Silicones. *Journal of Macromolecular Science Part A Chemistry*, Vol. A4, No. 3, pp. 529-544, May 1970.

Broz, M.E., VanderHart, D.L., and Washburn, N.R., Structure and mechanical properties of poly(D,L-lactic acid)/poly(ε-caprolactone) blends. *Biomaterials*, Vol. 24, pp. 4181-4190, 2003.

Eberhart, R.C., Huo, H.-H., and Nelson, K., Cardiovascular Materials. *MRS Bulletin*, Vol. 16, pp. 50-54, September 1991.

Engelberg, I., and Kohn, J., Physico-mechanical properties of degradable polymers used in medical applications: a comparative study. *Biomaterials*, Vol. 12, pp. 292-304, April 1991.

Ertel, S.I., and Kohn, J., Evaluation of a series of tyrosine-derived polycarbonates as degradable biomaterials. *Journal of Biomedical Materials Research*, Vol. 28, pp. 919-930, 1994.

Gomes, M.E., and Reis, R.L., Biodegradable polymers and composites in biomedical applications: from catgut to tissue engineering. Part 1: Available systems and their properties. *International Materials Reviews*, Vol. 49, No. 5, pp. 261-273, 2004.

Gunatillake, P.A., Martin, D.J., Meijs, G.F., McCarthy, S.J., and Adhikari, R., Designing Biostable Polyurethane Elastomers for Biomedical Implants. *Australian Journal of Chemistry*, Vol. 56, pp. 545-557, 2003.

Gursel, I., Balcik, C., Arica, Y., Akkus, O., Akkus, N., and Hasirci, V., Synthesis and mechanical properties of interpenetrating networks of polyhydroxybutyrate-*co*-hydroxyvalerate and polyhydroxyethyl methacrylate. *Biomaterials*, Vol. 19, No. 13, pp. 1137-1143, 1998.

Hoffman, A.S., Environmentally Sensitive Polymers and Hydrogels: "Smart" Biomaterials. *MRS Bulletin*, Vol. 16, pp. 42-46, September 1991.

Jacoby, M., Custom-Made Biomaterials. *Science & Technology*, Vol. 79, No. 6, pp. 30-35, 2001.

Jarvik, R.K., The Total Artificial Heart. *Scientific American*, Vol. 244, No. 1, pp. 74-80, January 1981.

Katz, J., Developments in Medical Polymers for Biomaterials Applications. *Medical Device & Diagnostic Industry*, pp. 122-133, January 2001.

Krause, W., and Mathis, R.S., Fatigue properties of acrylic bone cements: Review of the literature. *Journal of Biomedical Materials Research: Applied Biomaterials*, Vol. 22, No. A1, pp. 37-53, 1988.

Kurtz, S.M., Pruitt, L., Jewett, C.W., Crawford, R.P., Crane, D.J., and Edidin, A.A., The yielding, plastic flow, and fracture behavior of ultra-high molecular weight polyethylene used in total joint replacements. *Biomaterials*, Vol. 19, No. 21, pp. 1989-2003, 1998.

Langer, R., Drug Delivery Systems. *MRS Bulletin*, Vol. 16, pp. 47-49, September 1991.

Lewis, G., Fatigue Testing and Performance of Acrylic Bone-Cement Materials: State-of-the-Art Review. *Journal of Biomedical Materials Research Part B: Applied Biomaterials*, Vol. 66B, pp. 457-486, 2003.

Lewis, G., Polyethylene Wear in Total Hip and Knee Athroplasties. *Journal of Biomedical Materials Research (Applied Biomaterials)*, Vol. 38, pp. 55-75, 1997.

Lewis, G., Properties of Acrylic Bone Cement: State of the Art Review. *Journal of Biomedical Materials Research (Applied Biomaterials)*, Vol. 38, pp. 155-182, 1997.

Middleton, J.C., and Tipton, A.J., Synthetic biodegradable polymers as orthopedic devices. *Biomaterials*, Vol. 21, pp. 2335-2346, 2000.

Mikos, A.G., and Temenoff, J.S., Formation of highly porous biodegradable scaffolds for tissue engineering. *Electronic Journal of Biotechnology*, Vol. 3, No. 2, pp. 114-119, http://www.ejbiotechnology.info/content/vol3/issue2/full/5/5.pdf, 15 August 2000.

Miller, H., Making Sense of Plastics and Their Properties. *Medical Device & Diagnostic Industry*, pp. 98-104, May 2004.

Moukwa, M., The Development of Polymer-Based Biomaterials Since the 1920s. *JOM*, Vol. 49, No. 2, pp. 46-50.

Parker, S., Martin, D., and Braden, M., Soft acrylic resin materials containing a polymerisable plasticizer I: mechanical properties. *Biomaterials*, Vol. 19, No. 18, pp. 1695-1701, 1998.

Pêgo, A.P., Poot, A.A., Grijpma, D.W., and Feijen, J., Physical properties of high molecular weight 1,3-trimethylene carbonate and D,L-lactide copolymers. *Journal of Materials Science: Materials in Medicine*, Vol. 14, pp. 767-773, 2003.

Petrini, P., Farè, S., Piva, A., and Tanzi, M.C., Design, synthesis and properties of polyurethane hydrogels for tissue engineering. *Journal of Materials Science: Materials in Medicine*, Vol. 14, pp. 683-686, 2003.

Roe, R.-J., Grood, E.S., Shastri, R., Gosselin, C.A., and Noyes, F.R., Effect of radiation sterilization and aging on ultrahigh molecular weight polyethylene. *Journal of Biomedical Materials Research*, Vol. 15, pp. 209-230, 1981.

Seal, B.L., Otero, T.C., and Panitch, A., Polymeric biomaterials for tissue and organ regeneration. *Materials Science and Engineering R*, Vol. 34, pp. 147-230, 2001.

Shieh, S.-J., Zimmerman, M.C., and Parsons, J.R., Preliminary characterization of bioresorbable and nonresorbable synthetic fibers for the repair of soft tissue injuries. *Journal of Biomedical Materials Research*, Vol. 24, pp. 789-808, 1990.

Smoluk, G.R., How to use time-dependent property data. *Modern Plastics*, Vol. 41, pp. 119-122, 126, 128, 130, 190, 192, August, 1964.

Spaans, C.J., De Groot, J.H., Belgraver, V.W., and Pennings, A.J., A new biomedical polyurethane with a high modulus based on 1,4-butanediisocyanate and ε-caprolactone. *Journal of Materials Science: Materials in Medicine*, Vol. 9, pp. 675-678, 1998.

Tighe, B.J., The Design of Polymers for Contact Lens Applications. *The British Polymer Journal*, Vol. 8, pp. 71-77, September 1976.

Ward, R., Segmented Polyurethanes for Medical Applications: History, Present, and Future, http://www.polymertech.com/pubs/abstract_1.html.

Wichterle, O., and Lim, D., Hydrophilic Gels for Biological Use. *Nature*, Vol. 185, pp. 117-118, 1960.

Composites

Abu Bakar, M.S., Cheang, P., and Khor, K.A., Tensile properties and microstructural analysis of spheroidized hydroxyapatite-poly(etheretherketone) biocomposites. *Materials Science and Engineering*, Vol. A345, pp. 55-63, 2003.

Adams, D., Williams, D.F., and Hill, J., Carbon Fiber-Reinforced Carbon as a Potential Implant Material. *Journal of Biomedical Materials Research*, Vol. 12, pp. 35-42, 1978.

Cerrai, P., Guerra, G.D., Tricoli, M., Krajewski, A., Guicciardi, S., Ravaglioli, A., Maltinti, S., and Masetti, G., New composites of hydroxyapatite and bioresorbable macromolecular material. *Journal of Materials Science: Materials in Medicine*, Vol. 10, pp. 283-289, 1999.

Bigi, A., Panzavolta, S., and Roveri, N., Hydroxyapatite-gelatin films: a structural and mechanical characterization. *Biomaterials*, Vol. 19, No. 7-9, pp. 739-744, 1998.

Brook, I.M., and Hatton, P.V., Glass-ionomers: bioactive implant materials. *Biomaterials*, Vol. 19, pp. 565-571, 1998.

Chang, F.-K., Perez, J.L., and Davidson, J.A., Stiffness and strength tailoring of a hip prosthesis made of advanced composite materials. *Journal of Biomedical Materials Research*, Vol. 24, pp. 873-899, 1990.

Chen, F., Wang, Z.-C., and Lin, C.-J., Preparation and characterization of nano-sized hydroxyapatite particles and hydroxyapatite/chitosan nano-composite for use in biomedical materials. *Materials Letters*, Vol. 57, pp. 858-861, December 2002.

Christel, P.S., The Applications of Carbon Fiber-Reinforced Carbon Composites (CRFC) in Orthopedic Surgery. *CRC Critical Reviews in Biocompatibility*, Vol. 2, No. 3, pp. 189-218, 1986.

Daniels, A.U., Chang, M.K.O., Andriano, K.P., and Heller, J., Mechanical Properties of Biodegradable Polymers and Composites Proposed for Internal Fixation of Bone. *Journal of Applied Biomaterials*, Vol. 1, pp. 57-78, 1990.

Fu, Y., Yan, B., Loh, N.L., Sun, C.Q., and Hing, P., Characterization and tribological evaluation of MW-PACVD diamond coatings deposited on pure titanium. *Materials Science and Engineering*, Vol. A282, pp. 38-48, 2000.

González, P., Serra, J., Liste, S., Chiussi, S., León, B., Pérez-Amor, M., Martinez-Fernández, J., Arellano-López, A.R., and Varela-Feria, F.M., New biomorphic SiC ceramics coated with bioactive glass for biomedical applications. *Biomaterials*, Vol. 24, pp. 4827-4832, 2003.

Gilbert, J.L., Ney, D.S., and Lautenschlager, E.P., Self-reinforced composite poly(methyl methacrylate): static and fatigue properties. *Biomaterials*, Vol. 16, No. 14, pp. 1043-1055, 1995.

Ignatius, A.A., Wolf, S., Augat, P., and Claes, L.E., Composites made of rapidly resorbable ceramics and poly(lactide) show adequate mechanical properties for use as bone substitute materials. *Journal of Biomedical Materials Research*, Vol. 57, pp. 126-131, 2001.

Imai, T., Watari, F., Yamagata, S., Kobayashi, M., Nagayama, K., Toyoizumi, Y. and Nakamura, S., Mechanical properties and aesthetics of FRP orthodontic wire fabricated by hot drawing. *Biomaterials*, Vol. 19, No. 23, pp. 2195-2200, 1998.

Juhasz, J.A., Best, S.M., Brooks, R., Kawashita, M., Miyata, N., Kokubo, T., Nakamura, T., and Bonfield, W., Mechanical properties of glass-ceramic A-W-polyethylene composites: effect of filler content and particle size. *Biomaterials*, Vol. 25, pp. 949-955, 2004.

Kazanci, M., Cohn, D., Marom, G., Migliaresi, C., and Pegoretti, A., Fatigue characterization of polyethylene fiber reinforced polyolefin biomedical composites. *Composites: Part A*, Vol. 33, pp. 453-458, 2002.

Kettunen, J., Mäkeläa, Miettinen, H., Nevalainen, T., Heikkilä, M., Pohjonen, T., Törmälä, P., and Rokkanen, P.; Mechanical properties and strength retention of carbon fibre-reinforced liquid crystalline polymer (LCP/CF) composite: An experimental study on rabbits. *Biomaterials*, Vol. 19, No. 14, pp. 1219-1228, 1998.

Manhart, J., Kunzelmann, K.-H., Chen, H.Y., and Hickel, R., Mechanical Properties of New Composite Restorative Materials. *Journal of Biomedical Materials Research (Applied Biomaterials)*, Vol. 53, pp. 353-361, 2000.

Park, H.C., Liu, Y.K., and Lakes, R.S., The Material Properties of Bone-Particle Impregnated PMMA. *Journal of Biomechanical Engineering*, Vol. 108, pp. 141-148, May 1986.

Pilliar, R.M., Blackwell, R., MacNab, I., and Cameron, H.U., Carbon Fiber-Reinforced Bone Cement in Orthopedic Surgery. *Journal of Biomedical Materials Research*, Vol. 10, pp. 893-906, 1976.

Porter, B.D., Oldham, J.B., He, S.-L., Zobitz, M.E., Payne, R.G., An, K.N., Currier, B.L., Mikos, A.G., and Yaszemski, M.J., Mechanical Properties of a Biodegradable Bone Regeneration Scaffold, *Journal of Biomechanical Engineering*, Vol. 122, pp. 286-288, June 2000.

Pourdeyhimi, B., and Wagner, H.D., Elastic and ultimate properties of acrylic bone cement reinforced with ultra-high-molecular-weight polyethylene fibers. *Journal of Biomedical Materials Research*, Vol. 23, pp. 63-80, 1989.

Ramakrishna, S., Mayer, J., Wintermantel, E., and Leong, K.W., Biomedical applications of polymer-composite materials: a review. *Composites Science and Technology*, Vol. 61, pp. 1189-1224, 2001.

Roeder, R.K., Sproul, M.M., and Turner, C.H., Hydroxyapatite whiskers provide improved mechanical properties in reinforced polymer composites. *Journal of Biomedical Materials Research*, Vol. 67A, No. 3, pp. 801-812, 2003.

Sclippa, E., and Piekarski, K., Carbon Fiber Reinforced Polyethylene for Possible Orthopedic Uses, *Journal of Biomedical Materials Research*, Vol. 7, pp. 59-70, 1973.

Shinzato, S., Nakamura, T., Kokubo, T., and Kitamura, Y., Composites consisting of poly(methyl methacrylate) and alumina powder: An evaluation of their mechanical and biological properties. *Journal of Biomedical Materials Research*, Vol. 60, pp. 585-591, 2002.

Silva, V.V., Lameiras, F.S., and Domingues, R.Z., Microstructural and mechanical study of zirconia-hydroxyapatite (ZH) composite ceramics for biomedical applications. *Composites Science and Technology*, Vol. 61, pp. 301-310, 2001.

Tancred, D.C., McCormack, B.A.O., and Carr, A.J., A quantitative study of the sintering and mechanical properties of hydroxyapatite/phosphate glass composites. *Biomaterials*, Vol. 19, No. 19, pp. 1735-1743, 1998.

Thompson, I.D., and Hench, L.L., Mechanical properties of bioactive glasses, glass-ceramics and composites. *Proceedings of the Institution of Mechanical Engineers*, Vol. 212, No. 2, pp. 127-136, 1998.

Vail, N.K., Swain, L.D., Fox, W.C., Aufdlemorte, T.B., Lee, G., and Barlow, J.W., Materials for biomedical applications. *Materials and Design*, Vol. 20, pp. 123-132, 1999.

Biomaterials-related Databases

Berman, H. M., Olson, W. K., Beveridge, D. L., Westbrook, J., Gelbin, A., Demeny, T., Hsieh, S.-H., Srinivasan, A. R., and Schneider, B.: The Nucleic Acid Database: A Comprehensive Relational Database of Three-Dimensional Structures of Nucleic Acids. *Biophysical Journal*, Vol. 63, pp. 751-759, 1992. Maintained online at: http://ndbserver.rutgers.edu/.

Berman, H.M, Westbrook, J., Feng, Z., Gilliland, G., Bhat, T.N., Weissig, H., Shindyalov, I.N., and Bourne, P.E.: The Protein Data Bank. *Nucleic Acids Research*, 28 pp. 235-242, 2000. Maintained online at: http://www.rcsb.org/pdb/.

Gilliland, G.L., Tung, M., Blakeslee, D.M. and Ladner, J. 1994. The Biological Macromolecule Crystallization Database, Version 3.0: New Features, Data, and the NASA Archive for Protein Crystal Growth Data. *Acta Crystallogr.* D50 408-413. Maintained online at: http://wwwbmcd.nist.gov:8080/bmcd/bmcd.html.

O'Brien, W.J., University of Michigan Biomaterials Properties Database. http://www.lib.umich.edu/dentlib/Dental_tables/intro.html. 45 tables of biomaterials properties drawn from 244 references. Primarily dental materials.

ASTM Biomaterials Standards – all are from: *Annual Book of ASTM Standards, Vol. 13.01*; **West Conshohocken, PA: American Society for Testing and Materials, 2000.**

F67-95 Unalloyed Titanium for Surgical Implant Applications (3 pp.)

F75-98 Cobalt-28 Chromium-6 Molybdenum Casting Alloy and Cast Products for Surgical Implants (UNS R30075) (3)

F90-97 Wrought Cobalt-20 Chromium-15 Tungsten-10 Nickel Alloy for Surgical Implant Applications (UNS R30605) (3)

F136-98 Wrought Titanium – 6Aluminum – 4Vanadium ELI (Extra Low Interstitial) Alloy (UNS R56401) for Surgical Implant Applications (3)

F138-97 Wrought 18 Chromium-14 Nickel-2.5 Molybdenum Stainless Steel Bar and Wire for Surgical Implants (UNS S31673) (4)

F139-45 Wrought-18 Chromium-14 Nickel-2.5 Molybdenum Stainless Sheet and Strip for Surgical Implants (UNS S31673) (3)

F451-99a Acrylic Bone Cement (7)

F560-98 Unalloyed Tantalum for Surgical Implant Applications (UNS R05200, UNS R05400) (3)

F562-95 Wrought Cobalt-35 Nickel-20 Chromium-10 Molybdenum Alloy for Surgical Implant Applications (3)

F563-95 Wrought Cobalt-Nickel-Chromium-Molybdenum-Tungsten-Iron Alloy for Surgical Implant Applications (3)

F603-00 High-Purity Dense Aluminum Oxide for Medical Application (3)

F648-98 Ultra-High-Molecular-Weight Polyethylene Powder and Fabricated Form for Surgical Implants (6)

F688-95 Wrought Cobalt-35 Nickel-20 Chromium-10 Molybdenum Alloy Plate, Sheet, and Foil for Surgical Implants (3)

F702-98a Polysulfone Resin for Medical Applications (4)

F799-99 Cobalt-28Chromium-6Molybdenum Alloy Forgings for Surgical Implants (UNS R31537, R31538, R31539) (3)

F881-94 Silicone Elastomer Facial Implants (3)

F899-95 Stainless Steel Billet, Bar, and Wire for Surgical Instruments (6)

F961-96 Cobalt-35 Nickel-20 Chromium-10 Molybdenum Alloy Forgings for Surgical Implants [UNS R30035] (3)

F1058-97 Wrought Cobalt-Chromium-Nickel-Molybdenum-Iron Alloys for Surgical Implant Applications [UNS R 30003 and UNS R 30008] (4)

F1091-91 (Reapproved 1996) Wrought Cobalt-20 Chromium-15 Tungsten-10 Nickel Alloy Surgical Fixation Wire [UNS R30605] (2)

F1108-97a Titanium-6 Aluminum-4 Vanadium Alloy Castings for Surgical Implants [UNS R56406] (3)

F1295-97a Wrought Titanium-6 Aluminum-7 Niobium Alloy for Surgical Implant Applications [UNS R56700] (3)

F1314-95 Wrought Nitrogen Strengthened-22 Chromium-12.5 Nickel-5 Manganese-2.5 Molybdenum Stainless Steel Bar and Wire for Surgical Implants (3)

F1341-99 Unalloyed Titanium Wire UNS R50250, UNS R50400, UNS R50550, UNS R50700, for Surgical Implant Applications (3)

F1350-96 Wrought 18 Chromium-14 Nickel-2.5 Molybdenum Stainless Steel Surgical Fixation Wire (UNS S31673) (2)

F1472-99 Wrought Titanium – 6Aluminum – 4Vanadium Alloy for Surgical Implant Applications (UNS R56400) (4)

F1537-94 Wrought Cobalt-28 Chromium-6 Molybdenum Alloy for Surgical Implants (3)

F1579-98 Polyaryletherketone (PAEK) Resins for Surgical Implant Applications (6)

F1586-95 Wrought Nitrogen Strengthened-21 Chromium-10 Nickel-3 Manganese-2.5 Molybdenum Stainless Steel Bar for Surgical Implants (3)

F1713-96 Wrought Titanium-13Niobium-13Zirconium Alloy for Surgical Implant Applications (4)

F1813-97 Wrought Titanium 12 Molybdenum – 6 Zirconium – 2 Iron Alloy For Surgical Implant Applications (3)

F1873-98 High-Purity Dense Yttria Tetragonal Zirconium Oxide Polycrystal (Y-TZP) for Surgical Implant Applications (3)

F1876-98 Polyetherketoneetherketoneketone (PEKEKK) Resins for Surgical Implant Applications (4)

Lightning Source UK Ltd.
Milton Keynes UK
UKHW02n0829150818
327258UK00006B/17/P